*Quest for a Black Theology*

# QUEST FOR A BLACK THEOLOGY

*Edited by*
*James J. Gardiner, SA*
*and*
*J. Deotis Roberts, Sr.*

A Pilgrim Press Book
*Philadelphia*

Chapter 6, "Jesus, the Liberator" originally
appeared as a paper in *Andover Newton Quarterly
Review*, Vol. X (3), January 1970, and is reprinted
with permission of the author.

# Contents

# PREFACE

Five of the six essays which comprise this collection were originally presented at an interdenominational conference devoted to an exploration of the "Black Church/Black Theology" phenomenon. The conference, which was jointly sponsored by the Graymoor Ecumenical Institute and the Georgetown University Department of Theology, was held on May 2 and 3, 1969 in Washington, D.C.

Inspiration for the conference came from Dr. J. Deotis Roberts, coeditor of this volume, who at the time of our first meeting was a lecturer on the faculty of the School of Theology at Catholic University in Washington, D.C. When presented with the original idea for the conference, Dr. Roberts responded enthusiastically and promised his cooperation. Throughout the many weeks of planning he offered many invaluable suggestions and criticisms. Any success attributable either to the conference or to this volume is due in large measure to his efforts.

Appreciation must likewise be expressed to the Rev. Ralph Thomas, SA, director of the Graymoor Ecumenical Institute with headquarters in Garrison, N.Y., and to the Rev. William C. McFadden, S.J., chairman of the Department of Theology at Georgetown University in Washington, D.C. Both these men, by their cooperation, insight, and encouragement, made the conference a realizable possibility.

As coordinator for the original conference and coeditor of this volume, it was also my pleasure to work with Mrs. Mildred Wyatt, secretary of the Graymoor Ecumenical Institute and with Dennis Polanco, SA, and Kenneth Stofft, SA, both of the Atonement Seminary in Washington, D.C.

James J. Gardiner, SA

Akron, Ohio
December 3, 1970

# INTRODUCTION

After centuries of neglect, black theology is coming into its own. Just as the "invisible church" of the black man preceded the visible organization, even so an indigenous black theology has appeared here and there in sermon, spiritual, and black folk expression. Much of the data for a black theology has been in the oral tradition. It has not appeared before in writing. It appears now for the first time as a clearly organized and articulate expression of beliefs. Theology as "reflection upon the Christian experience in black" is a new thing.

Not all the writers of essays in this volume claim to be "school" theologians. Some are "folk" theologians. Some are ethicists. Others may prefer to be known as churchmen. All are concerned with black consciousness, pride, power, and liberation. The volume is enriched by its variety.

Albert B. Cleage, Jr. has been called the "prophet of the black nation." He is an exponent of the "Black Messiah" as an archsymbol of the black religious revolution. He is an advocate of "separatism" in the form of religious nationalism. His essay is a prime illustration of a point of view which has wide acceptance among Blacks who have given up on integration as a solution to race relations. Some Blacks have a problem with the "Black Madonna" for sociological as well as theological reasons. Sociologically, the black madonna is associated with the female-headed family pattern. This family pattern has resulted from oppression in a white racist society and is not of African origin. It is believed by these critics that this pattern of family life must be overcome if black nationalism is to be a success. Therefore, Cleage's Shrine of the Black Madonna together with the symbol of the black madonna convey the wrong message. Theologically, most Blacks are Protestant (Methodist or Baptist). The black madonna, associated in their minds with the meaning of the virgin Mary for Roman Catholics, is not attractive to them. The black Messiah, if interpreted existentially, helps Blacks overcome their identity crisis and can become a powerful symbol of faith. If, on the other hand, it is understood in the literal-historical manner of Cleage, it presents a real problem for biblical scholars as well as theologians. Black lay Christians are obviously confused, for it shatters their literal-infallible understanding of scripture. The Bible, "a pan-Afro-American book," speaks to all segments of the black population. Cleage is able to overcome much of the criticism aimed at him by scholars, for he is "a man of the people." His position is a bridge between the religion of Black Power or black religious nationalism and Afro-American Christianity. His essay is a real contribution to a folk expression of black theology. Here we use "folk" in an appreciative sense, for we believe Cleage is able to reflect upon aspects of the black experience unavailable to academic theologians. Without his contribution our volume would be even more incomplete.

Joseph R. Washington, Jr. has for several years been an articulate spokesman for black religion. He has been a pioneer in that he described black religion before it became popular to do so. In a controversial book, *Black Religion,* Washington not only dared to be critical of black folk religion, he even suggested that black churches should renounce their Jesusology and go out of business. His "honeymoon" with white religion was short-lived, however. The course of events in the area of race led him to write *Politics of God* and *Black-White Power Subreption.* In these latter works, Washington has wormed his way back into the black religious tradition. Some black militants, some of whom are churchmen, hold Washington in suspicion if not in contempt. Washington's first book was a pacesetter, however. He must be recognized for his insights in spite of his rapid changes. The essay in this volume explores the "soul" experience in black religion. It is a real contribution to the sociology of black religious experience. He provides materials unavailable in his larger works or in the "rash" of materials being published by other black writers.

Walter L. Yates has explored the history of "God-consciousness" in the black church. His essay is rich in historical material. He traces the roots of black religious experience in Egypt, West Africa, and through our "Afro-American past." He sees "God-consciousness" as "a stabilizing creative force in the life of man"—even the black American. His account of the history of the black church provides a historical background for an appreciation of the contribution of Blacks to the Christian movement. Yates enables us to see black church history in the context of world history as well. Few Blacks have adequate knowledge of both the history of Christianity and Afro-American Christianity to bring the two together as he has done. He is a mature researcher, a careful and thoughtful organizer of his materials. Due to the urgent need for the subject matter at his fingertips, we encourage him to make a more frequent and abundant contribution on the printed page. What he can offer us may not be the most popular, but it is likely to be the most lasting contribution to our self-understanding as black Christians. We are pleased to have this essay and urge the reader to give careful and thoughtful consideration to what he has presented.

As former teacher, friend, and consultant to Fr. James Gardiner, coeditor of this volume and organizer of the Georgetown Conference on Black Church/Black Theology, the present writer shares an overview with him of the entire session. My own essay was the result of preliminary reflection upon the nature and scope of a black theology. Therefore, "Black Consciousness in Theological Perspective" is a "position paper" on the subject. It has been offered here in its original form because it is how I viewed the beginnings of a radically new departure in theological discourse. It does raise many of the crucial issues to be treated in any theological understanding of the black religious experience. It begins "construction" of the doctrines of God and man combining black experience with the Christian creed. It marks a break with my own theological past and clearly points to a direction which I have followed in my version of a black theology which is, in some respects, different from some of my soul brothers, i.e., Cone, Cleage, Washington. Some observers noted that "reconciliation" as well as "liberation" emerged in this essay. I am pleased that reconciliation should have been so natural, even if liberation was consciously being sought. This essay was for me "a maiden voyage in an uncharted ocean," but it is a "beginning" without which no further voyage would have been possible. The reader will discover many of the right questions and few of the right answers. This essay has been a great stimulus for my subsequent reflection upon black theology. If it provokes constructive criticism, it will have served a worthy purpose. Its "end" is a beginning.

Preston N. Williams enters the discussion as a social ethicist and treats "the ethics of Black Power." At the time Williams made this contribution, he had not written a major work on the subject. Several of his articles continue to appear. These cast significant light upon our understanding of the black religious experience. Williams describes the nature of the separation between Blacks and Whites, even within the church. He goes on to define Black Power and what it should mean for black Christians. As the cochairman of the Theological Commission of the National Committee of Black Churchmen, Williams is optimistic about the affirmative use of black awareness through black ecumenism. He condemns the "conscienceless power" of white Christians who have exploited the black man's desire to integrate through nonviolent means. He makes it clear that Blacks must accept their humanity before human life can become more human for them. This, Williams believes, requires "a redefinition of soul" and "a reinterpretation of the Christian heritage." He points to the insensitivity of Whites in the use of power. The criticism of White Power, in church and society, is the proper mission of the black church. Williams is seeking "the ethical implications" of Black Power. He relies very heavily upon the statements of the National Committee of Black Churchmen. His essay has the advantage of combining his personal reflections with those of the fellowship most representative of "black ecumenism" at the present time.

Joseph A. Johnson, Jr. combines churchmanship and scholarship. He ascended the bishopric from a chair of New Testament. He serves with Preston Williams as cochairman of the Theological Commission of the National Committee of Black Churchmen. His essay combines careful scholarship with a sensitivity from the "field." His contribution to "a black Christology" is one of the finest and most creative statements on the subject available. Johnson was not a participant at the Georgetown Conference. It is a great honor to have his paper included here. It has greatly enriched the volume and expanded the knowledge of our quest.

All the writers of essays in this volume are speaking to the "mood ebony" against the background of their understanding of the Christian faith. All are aware of the urgency of their task and have given of their knowledge and experience to make this expression worthwhile. This is a much-needed volume. It points to the variety of viewpoints within the black church. The writers come from different backgrounds and experiences. But what we really have is a "diversity-in-unity." What appears as "a divided mind" among these several black writers will be wrongly understood if it is viewed as more than "a family quarrel." All Blacks who speak here are painfully aware of the need for black liberation. Without freedom, black men will be able to make little sense or use of the claims of the Christian faith. Joseph Washington speaks for all of us when he describes black theology as a theology of freedom.

It has been a wholesome experience to work with Father James Gardiner of the Society of the Atonement. As chairman of the conference and as representative of the Graymoor Ecumenical Institute, Father Gardiner has shown a genuine interest in both ecumenics and race relations. This institute together with the Department of Theology of Georgetown University, made this lecture-discussion available to a nationwide assembly of laity and clergy of many faiths. It is rewarding to work with men of goodwill toward that reconciliation which is in Christ.

> J. Deotis Roberts, Sr.
> Swarthmore College
> Swarthmore, Pennsylvania
> Spring 1970

*Quest for a Black Theology*

# Chapter One

# THE BLACK MESSIAH AND
# THE BLACK REVOLUTION

*Albert B. Cleage, Jr.*

In 1954 the United States Supreme Court ended its "separate but equal" doctrine and declared that inherent in the legal segregation of black people is a white *declaration of black inferiority* which automatically renders any education received by a black child within this framework psychologically damaging and consequently inferior. Apparently the schools of America were being ordered to desegregate "with all deliberate" speed in order that black people could proceed to develop a positive new self-image. The effects of the court order upon black people were instantaneous and profound. Desegregation has not yet been accomplished but interpreting the court's decision as a basic legal revocation of the white man's *declaration of black inferiority*, black people began a frantic struggle to realize instant integration in all areas of life. Although segregation remains, participation in the black struggle has enabled the black man to reject the white man's *declaration of black inferiority* and has actually served to bring into being the positive self-image which the Supreme Court decision implied could only come with the ending of segregation, signaling the white man's rejection of his own *declaration of black inferiority*. A white court naturally assumed that initiative in the long, slow, and difficult process of changing the relationship between white people and black people must come from white people. This assumption was reflected in the nonlegal determination that desegregation should proceed "with all deliberate speed." Segregation in public education was declared illegal and unconstitutional but would be ended only as speedily as white people could be persuaded to permit it to be ended. Few people then realized that if white people were not willing to change their definition of black people, then black people could force a new relationship by changing their definition of themselves and forcing white people to deal with them on a new basis. Let us trace the steps by which this strange revolution in the thinking of an oppressed people came to pass. In its 1954 decision the Court laid a foundation for social change of which it could not then have been aware, and for which it cannot now be held responsible. Only God in his infinite wisdom could have foreseen the direction in which this decision would drive black people.

The lives of black people in America were grounded in a dream of integration. African culture had been uprooted and destroyed, and even language and religion had been forgotten. Africans of the diaspora had become a people without a past. With the will to survive they adjusted to a new reality and the demands of their powerlessness. They identified with the white slave master, his white institutions, and his white culture. Each black man struggled to survive by aping his white master and seeking his approval. The only escape from powerlessness and the indignities of inferiority here on earth appeared to be integration with the powerful and therefore superior white master. The effects of the 1954 Supreme Court decision upon black people can be understood only in this light. The integration of which an enslaved black people had dreamed now seemed possible. The nation's highest tribunal had declared that integration was now the law of the land and segregation was no longer legally acceptable. Black people took the Supreme Court decision and made of it a heroic declaration of equality. The Supreme Court had not intended to say as much as black people read into the decision. But the decision did say that segregation in public education was no longer legal, and that with all deliberate speed changes must be made so that black people could have an integrated education. Black people drew the rather logical conclusion that if segregation in education is wrong because there are inequities inherent in the fact of segregation, then segregation itself is wrong and segregation everywhere must be abolished immediately. So the beginning of the black revolution was the dream of integration. Black people took the

Supreme Court decision seriously and began the struggle to realize instant integration.

Black college students in the South proceeded to try to implement the Supreme Court's decision by protesting against all kinds of segregation. Black people wanted immediate integration in all areas of life. So we had the sit-ins, the wade-ins, the kneel-ins, and the freedom rides, all over the South. Militant young black people and older black people were united in a common effort to realize total and complete integration. So the movement came into being, as a struggle to realize immediate integration. Today's militant black leaders were yesterday's integrationists. Stokely Carmichael was an integrationist and cooperated with Martin Luther King, Jr., the messiah of the integrationist movement. Rap Brown was part of the student nonviolent integration.

The integration movement dominated the scene in America for a number of years following the 1954 Supreme Court decision. It seems strange when we look back from where we are now to realize that in 1954 black people took seriously the possibility of integration. It can only be understood if we remember that black people had believed in the possibility of integration through all the misery of their American bondage. Always there was the hope that integration would offer an escape from powerlessness and oppression. Forty to 100 million black people were killed during the slave trades—being captured in Africa, being taken to the slave ships, on board slave ships, on the slave block, and on the plantations. Yet during all this horror and brutality, black people still looked forward to the time when they would be integrated with their oppressors. So the dream of integration was part of the black experience.

During this whole period black people felt that the reason integration was so slow in coming was really the fault of black people themselves. White people were good, they were kindly, they were well-intentioned, and their apparent brutality was necessary to prepare black people for integration. Even when millions of black people were being killed, they still felt that the white man was right and that they were wrong, and that they were engaged in a mysterious process of trying to become as much like their white oppressors as possible. Self-hatred was part of the black man's desire for integration. The black man's life in America constituted a process by which a proud African people were niggerized. The end of slavery and the rise of the Klan with the thousands of public lynchings which were condoned by the total community did not change the black man's faith in the goodness of white people. The little book *One Hundred Years of Lynching,* with the documented accounts of 5,000 lynchings from newspapers and other public documents, indicates the exquisite conditioning by which black men were psychologically destroyed. Three counties would come together for a lynching party with advance notices and press releases. People would meet at an appointed time and place and a black man would be lynched. The lynching was of the most brutal kind. The black man would be mutilated, killed slowly, and his body destroyed. Yet through all this, even when black people were forced to watch the brutality, they still believed that white people were good and that black people were bad, and that the only reason white people did these things was because of the badness of black people, and they still longed for integration.

With this kind of total identification with white people and desire to be accepted by them and to become part of their white world and its white institutions, the 1954 Supreme Court decision called into being a movement designed to accomplish instant integration. Black people really expected to see the walls of Jericho come tumbling down. The mobilization of white people to prevent integration was at first assumed to be the work of a few bad white men who did not represent the white community. Only gradually did it become obvious to black people that their interpretation of reality was false. The white man was not good. The white man had not been waiting for the black man to achieve a degree of perfection which would enable him to be accepted for integration. Actually the white man hated and despised black people. The white man was an enemy and all his institutions were enemy institutions. This was not an immediate revelation for black people. They didn't just wake up one morning realizing that they lived in a hostile land surrounded by enemies, who were determined to destroy them psychologically and physically if necessary. But gradually over a period of time, through situations which black people experienced personally or vicariously by way of television, black people came to the realization that white America is built upon a basic contradiction which excludes all black people from the American dream. White people hate black people and are committed to their oppression and exploitation.

On television black people would see a black mother taking a little black child through a howling savage white mob, into a school that had been integrated by law. The howling mob of white people organized to prevent this integration was part of the revelation which came to black people. These were not white people who had been released from insane asylums and penitentiaries for participation in a mob scene. They were the ordinary white people of the community—the deacons in the church, the boy scout leaders, the girl scout leaders, YMCA people, together they made up the mob. So, for black people it was a new experience. It was seeing suddenly that white people are united in the exclusion and total oppression of black people. The sit-in demonstrations where black people asked only for the privilege of eating a 10-cent hot dog at a lunch counter aroused the same communitywide defense of white supremacy. The television scene showing a huge white man knocking a black girl from a counter stool, kicking her, throwing mustard and catsup on her to the obvious glee of the white people who were present was part of the educational experience of black people. Only gradually did black people begin to break their identification and to realize that white people did not want integration, would not accept it, and would do anything to prevent it.

Black people began to seek a new reality upon which to build their lives. Obviously they had been living a lie and now somewhere in their black experience they must find something upon which they could build a life that was real. So black people began the painful struggle to discover a new black reality. Dr. King's integration movement had taken black people as far as he was equipped to lead them, and that was a long, long way. Dr. King took black people who were still stepping off the sidewalk in the presence of white people and set up face-to-face confrontations with White Power across the South. Through the absurd nonviolent and redemptive love tactic that Dr. King used, black people learned that they could stand up against white people and White Power, and that white people were not invincible. Dr. King moved across the South from one confrontation situation to another, preaching love but actually exposing the white man as he had never been exposed before. Black people began to see that there is no possibility of integration with white people because the white man is the black man's enemy.

Black people with their tremendous sense of forgiveness and love still tried to rationalize away the fact that all white people are in fact part of the same white system of oppression. They said bad white people are in the South, and good white people are in the North. Then Dr. King, as his last great contribution before his assassination, went to Chicago and proved conclusively that there is no such thing as good white people and bad white people and that white people make up one system of oppression and brutality. In Chicago there was exactly the same reaction as in the South: the total mobilization of the white community to block integration and the black man's freedom struggle. When some of the brothers marched into Cicero they revealed exactly the same face of white hatred, the same drooling idiotic violent response to the black man's most modest demands for equality. Obviously the march into Cicero was a symbolic march. Nobody wants to live in Cicero. The revelation was complete. Even the white people who didn't want to live in Cicero themselves didn't want any black people living there with them. And so the whole dramatic period of Dr. King's confrontations had come to a close. White people had finally revealed themselves to black people. Black people had finally gotten the message.

Today when black people talk about separatism, black pride, and doing their own thing, white people are shocked, and they ask, why do you black people hate us so? Why do you want to separate yourselves instead of being part of the body of Christ (if they are Christians) or of the nation (if they are politicians)? Why do you black people want to do this thing? You are destroying America. It took us a long time to accept reality, to understand that there are two Americas: one white and one black. White America has power; it controls the economics, the politics, the religion, and all the institutional structures of America. Then there is black America, which is powerless, in which the people control nothing, in which black people are enslaved. Black people do not control the politics of the communities in which they live. They do not control the economics of the communities in which they live. They do not control the culture, the education, the libraries. They do not control any of the institutions upon which their communities depend. They are a powerless, exploited, oppressed, and brutalized people. Two Americas. One black and one white. This then is the emerging reality for black people. We had to learn that it's not a matter of a white man's ideology. The problem does not grow out of the fact that some white people believe one thing and some believe another. It makes no difference; a white communist, a white Christian, a white socialist, a white middle-class politician, a white suburbanite, a white alcoholic on skid row have no real ideological differences insofar as black people are concerned.

Black people are oppressed because they are powerless and they are identifiable. They are oppressed by white people who have power and who control a system. It is necessary to understand then that a white person is part of this oppressive system, whether or not he engages in face-to-face brutality. You don't have to beat a black man to death to be involved in the destruction of black people. Teachers in schools, even those who think that they love little black children, and drive in from the suburbs because they want to teach little black children, are part of the psychological destruction of black people. A white teacher who teaches in a black school is a power symbol for a black child. And whatever love she has in her heart cannot in any way compensate for the effects of her presence. She teaches a little black child by her very presence that power in America is in the hands of white people. That even in a school the power symbols, the white teacher, the white principal, the white administrator indicate the basic and persuasive nature of White Power. Apart from the questions of motivation and power symbols, black schools are inferior because money is withheld from the education of black children in order that the education of white children may be improved. So if you live in a suburban community and there are no black children there, your little white child gets a better education because a little black child in a ghetto school is given less of an education. No matter where you work you have greater job security because you don't have to worry about real competition from black people because there's a ceiling on how far a black man can go. So wherever you are, even in the church, perhaps especially in the church, you have a privileged position. A black minister has a certain limited area in which he can function. A white minister does not have to worry about the competition of a black preacher. It is a privileged position that the white man has. It is a power position. It is difficult for white people to recognize this and accept it, because he who has power feels that his power has been divinely bestowed. He who is powerless also tends to feel that his powerlessness has been divinely bestowed as punishment for some mystical sin committed in the past.

Black people had much to learn and I think that we have only just begun the difficult struggle involved in facing reality. The truths which are basic for our new position sound strange when we say them aloud. First and inescapable is the simple fact that the white man is our enemy. This is important to the black church because a black theology must deal with this reality if it is going to be a theology which black people can accept. The white man is an enemy. To survive we must break our identification with the enemy. To survive we must escape from powerlessness. Somehow we must find some process by which we can build power. We must escape from powerlessness if we are to deal with a white enemy. To survive, we must reject the dream of integration which serves as the mechanism of our continuing enslavement. A black businessman feels that his business has very little significance because he is living in a mystical never-never land of integration that can never be. It is this suspended animation from which black people are now in the process of escaping. To escape from powerlessness we must reject the dreams of integration.

So everywhere today black people are enraged and white people are resentful. These are the two faces of America which we see everywhere. A black America which is powerless, in which black people are enraged and struggling to find a new black identity, struggling to escape from identification with white people, struggling for economic power, political power, and the power to control black communities. And a white America in which white people feel threatened and resentful. "Good, liberal" white people who have given so much for black people are the most outraged and resentful. They are the most afraid and they feel the most threatened. In a sense they built their lives on a lie just as black people did. To have that lie exploded shakes the foundation of their lives and destroys their reason for being. "Liberal, Christian" white people are the most threatened by the new emerging black man who wants to stand alone, to be a person, to be a black man, and to think as a black man and to live in terms of his struggle for power. White America and black America are locked in a never-ending power struggle. This is the reality with which we all must live.

In the midst of a black revolution in which black people are struggling for power, slave Christianity no longer meets their needs. Slave Christianity is the Christianity that old master gave black people back on the plantation. He defined Jesus, and showed pictures of Jesus with his flowing golden locks and his blue eyes. The obvious absurdity of the portrait never even occurred to black people. There was no way in the world Jesus could have looked like the pictures in the Bible, having been born in the part of the world reserved for black people by God. The whiteness of Jesus and Israel was basic to slave Christianity. Old master taught black people that God was primarily concerned with petty little sins (you don't fornicate, you don't smoke, you don't play cards, you don't drink). A petty morality too trivial for God's concern were the basic elements of slave Christianity. The whole idea of Christianity had to do with an individual kind of salvation. Two thousand years ago on Calvary a mystic event took place. Jesus was crucified, and somehow he rose from the dead. In this redemptive act, God made salvation possible for individuals who believed in all generations. This meant then that each individual must fight for his own little individual salvation. Black people took this slave Christianity and made of it an instrument for survival. They put into it a vitality which the white man did not have in his own church. They believed fervently because they needed to believe; they needed a dream of escape in a world in which there was no real possibility of escape. They could conceive of no way to end their oppression so they used this slave theology as one way of maintaining sanity. Slave Christianity made it possible for black people to survive. The slaves took the idea of going to heaven seriously. They took their pain and suffering to Jesus. The slave could stand anything that the white man did, saying, "The white man can beat me, he can rob me, he can cheat me, he can rape my wife and my daughters, he can do anything, but I can take it all to Jesus and I know that ultimately Jesus will triumph because through his sacrifice God has already redeemed me. So whatever the white man does I can accept." He went to church on Sunday and shouted with joy, running up and down the aisles in sheer ecstasy. The most effective Christian preaching in America was in black pulpits with ignorant black preachers preaching slave Christianity as no one in the world ever preached it before, to people who had to believe because they had no alternative for this mystical religious escape.

The black slave church was also destroying black people. Black people suffered discrimination because they were black. They were persecuted, they were brutalized, they were discriminated against, they were exploited, solely because they were black. And then in church on Sunday morning the black slave preacher, would say, "God is concerned about each one of you. You think that all week he hasn't been looking at you, but he's been watching everything that the white man has been doing to you. God knows what white people have done to you and someday he is going to shake them over hellfire. One of these days God is going to do for you what you can't do yourself. So get along with these white people as best as you can, because soon you are going to be taken up yonder to God and then you can sit at his right hand, and look down into hell where white people are roasting over hellfire." That was a beautiful message with simple basic eloquence and power about it. I only wish that it were true! But then you remember that black people had been working all week for nothing, being beaten up by policemen and exploited in every possible way. The preacher helped them to forget by telling them how beautiful it was going to be up there, and pretty soon they would be running up and down the aisles, shouting and screaming, and for the moment each individual escaped from his everyday problems, and for the moment was completely out of this world. The church and slave Christianity has perpetuated our individualism. We don't have any sense of being a people fighting our problems together. We're waiting for God to save us individually. We're running up and down the aisle shouting and singing and hoping that Jesus will speak to our individual needs, not the needs of black people. We do not really ask God to help us change the basic conditions under which black people live. This is the weakness of the black church. It was a survival instrument. It helped maintain sanity, but it destroyed the possibility of a united black liberation struggle. The black preacher preached escapism and individualism. He destroyed the possibility of black people fighting together to change oppressive conditions. There were exceptions. There was Nat Turner who was a black preacher who understood that the lynching of Jesus on Calvary two thousand years ago did not stop him from trying to kill white people who were oppressing his people. He was a black preacher who somehow saw the inadequacies and the contradictions of slave Christianity. But his revolt failed because some good Christian brother betrayed him along the way to guarantee his salvation in glory. As long as black people could see no possibility of changing the world, escapism was good old religion. It was all that a black preacher could preach to a black congregation. As long as there was no way for black people to change their condition it was natural to concentrate on the possibility of a good life after death.

As soon as black people began to see the world in which they lived realistically, they began to see white people as they really are—corrupt, brutal, and oppressive. When black people began to look at white people and see them as they were they said we can change this world ourselves, we don't have to wait for Jesus. And that marked the beginning of a whole new way of life for black people. Then black people began to try to change the world day by day, not waiting either for Jesus or for the redemption of white people. This new attitude could not fit into the slave church. The new black militant talked about people working together to change the black man's condition. The slave preacher still talked about sending individuals to heaven one by one. The two can't mix. In Harlem half a million black people crowd into thousands of little churches every Sunday, and nothing is done to change the black man's condition in New York City. The ineffectiveness of the black church is reflected in the condition of Harlem. The black church could change Harlem any day it offered black people leadership here on earth by bringing black people together. The white power structure has a vested interest in keeping slave Christianity alive. No one will ever organize a black community for united action as long as black preachers stand up on Sunday morning and take people to heaven one by one. As soon as black people began to conceive of the possibility of changing the world, the absolute necessity for a new interpretation of the Bible and a new black theology became obvious. Now there were other possible solutions. Black people could just leave the church, and I think many white people would rather that we did just that. But Christianity belongs to us. We are not going to give it up just because white people have messed it up.

So when we began to see that we could change the world we began to see that the church offered a broad institutional power base that could be useful in the black revolution. The only institution black people have is the church. We don't have anything else. All of our money is tied up in religious structures and a good part of our trained personnel is tied up in religious institutions. We cannot just turn and leave it. We need it in the liberation struggle. Which means that we must change the church radically. We must make the church relevant to the black revolution. The black revolution consists from day to day of those people who have severed their identification with white people, who realize that white people are the enemy, and are engaged in a struggle for power to control black communities. The black revolution must somehow take over the black church because the black revolution needs the black church. The black revolution will continue no matter what happens to the black church. But the black church can be helpful to the black revolution. Many young black militants think that the black church is too much trouble. They say that it is more trouble than it is worth. They would rather just leave it. But I am in it, I have a vested interest in it, and I am determined to take it along with the revolution. I am convinced that it can serve a valuable purpose if we will take the time to restructure it.

Everything must be restructured—its historical analysis, its biblical interpretation, its theology, its ritual, its preaching, everything. We can't just say we're going to change it a little bit, we're going to patch it up a little here and a little there. The whole basic Pauline interpretation of Christianity is historically false. The theology built on it has no relationship with the teachings of Jesus at all. You can ask, "How do you know?" I can reply, "That's a good question because none of us knows very much about what Jesus taught." All that we know about Jesus was filtered through the eyes of the early church after it had already been corrupted by the apostle Paul who was an Uncle Tom who wanted to identify with his white gentile Roman oppressors. Paul was very proud of his Roman citizenship although he was an oppressed Jew. Just like a black man today talking about his American citizenship. And I dare say that Paul's Roman citizenship did him just about as much good as a black man's American citizenship does him today. But that doesn't have anything to do with the way a man feels. Paul wanted to feel like a Roman. He wanted to be part of the pagan Roman world, so he took something that happened, the history and the person of Jesus and distorted them to make them acceptable to a pagan heathen world. There was some controversy about it. The disciples who remained in Jerusalem knew that he was preaching a false doctrine that had nothing at all to do with the Jesus with whom they had walked and talked. They tried to hold him accountable for his white corruptions. He tricked them just like people do today. He raised money from the churches he had organized and went back to Jerusalem with enough money to persuade the original disciples to overlook the fact that he was teaching a false doctrine. This is true. Paul does not follow in the footsteps of Jesus.

The black church must go back to the beginning and seek to rediscover the original teaching of Jesus and the nation Israel. There is very little historicity in the gospels and in the New Testament. In the Old Testament we have a little history intermingled with much fantasy and myth. Let's just admit that we don't have much, except insofar as we can understand the conditions out of which Jesus came and the role which he played in his day. We can find a few historical fragments in the Synoptic Gospels. We depend upon the Old Testament to validate the New Testament. Preachers don't quite know what to do with the Old Testament except to go back at Christmastime and find passages which prove that Jesus was the Messiah. All of which have nothing to do with Jesus. Essentially the Old Testament contradicts the New. The easy way to get around that of course is to say that the New Testament is an expansion and development and takes the Old Testament to new heights, which we also know is a lie. It says something entirely different. The New Testament does not take the Old Testament to new heights. It is a complete contradiction of the Old Testament, and Jesus came to fulfill the Old Testament.

We go back to the beginning of the Old Testament and we find mythology of course. Moses did not write the first five books of the Old Testament. At some point Israel became a nation. At some point the process began. We like to begin with Abraham. We have the basic outline of his wanderings. In the beginning he was a Chaldean. Most of you who have seen Chaldeans know that they are not nearly so white even to begin with as the pictures of Jesus in our Sunday school literature, and this Chaldean and his family wandered into Africa at the beginning of putting together the nation Israel. He went down into Egypt where his wife had an affair with pharaoh to save Abraham's neck. Pharaoh finally discovered the deception and ordered Abraham and Sarah out of Egypt. To avoid God's displeasure, he gave him gifts including animals, slaves, and concubines. Abraham continued his wandering. Sarah was unable to have a child, and so she suggested that he have a child by Hagar, an Egyptian servant girl. And so Ishmael, Abraham's heir, was born of an Egyptian slave, Hagar. Obviously the relationships were close and friendly. Later they tried to get rid of Hagar and Ishmael. But certainly the Jews did not have any racial prejudice in the sense that they held themselves apart from other peoples. Wherever they went they tended to mingle, to intermarry, and to become part of the people. So as Israel wandered in Africa Israel became blacker and blacker. Some of you may want to argue that the Egyptians were not black. That is a ridiculous argument which could only arise in America. Studies have been made which prove beyond a shadow of a doubt that most of the pharaohs were negroid. I use the word so you won't think that I am saying only "nonwhite." I'm talking about black. Most of the pharaohs had negroid blood that even now can be discovered by doing X rays of the mummies of the pharaohs. The percentage of pharaohs who obviously had negroid blood was markedly high in a study done recently by the University of Michigan Dental School. Studies of poor Egyptians indicate an even higher percentage as would be expected. The Egyptians were black. The intermingling of the Egyptians with Israel in the building of the nation Israel indicates that Israel was in the process of becoming black and everywhere that Israel went Israel grew blacker and blacker. Finally Joseph was sold into slavery and ended up back in Egypt. Israel went back into Egypt to escape from famine and settled there and became part of the people until "there arose a pharaoh who knew not Joseph." The mingling and intermixture is obvious. Then there were four hundred years of slavery. The Egyptians were the great slave traders of the ancient world and they made regular forays into the Sudan, into the land of the black people, and brought back slaves. And so in slavery in Egypt there were black people and there were the Israelites who were in the process of becoming black. For four hundred years they lived together and intermingled as slaves. At the time of their escape across the Red Sea, the black nation Israel was blacker than the Egyptians from whom they were fleeing.

Moses went off into Midian and married a black woman, the daughter of Jethro, and from Jethro, the high priest of Midian he borrowed the Yahweh religion which became the religion of the Israelites. Israel not only intermarried with the black peoples of Egypt and the Sudan but adopted the ideas and culture of black people. Moses brought back a concept of God from the Midianites. The God who spoke to Moses from the burning bush defined himself as the Midianite God. Jethro later visited Moses and gave him basic ideas of political organization. The Old Testament is the history of the development of a black nation. Perhaps you know many Jewish people today who do not look black. That's because the Jewish people in the Western world are the descendants of Jews who were converted to Judaism about one thousand years after the death of Jesus, in Europe, in Russia, and in other places in the white world. But even these "white Jews" retain physical signs of their black beginnings. A few communities have maintained an unbroken continuity since the fall of Jerusalem in A.D. 70. A Jewish community in India has descendants of the original black Jews who came to India directly from Israel, after the fall, and who are still black. The community also has some white Jews who migrated from Europe as merchants. There is constant conflict in this little Jewish community. The white Jews feel themselves superior to the black Jews. Particularly the white Jews don't want their daughters to marry the young black Jewish men. There are black Jews scattered throughout the world especially in Africa and in areas near to Israel. General Dayan's daughter recently complained in the world press that she was very upset because her house in Israel had depreciated in value because black Jews had purchased property on either side of her. The existence of black Jews is still a reality. White Jews are Zionists who needed Israel as a homeland, but are not of the bloodline of Abraham, Isaac, and Jacob.

Black Jews, as they became a people in their wandering, developed basic ideas which were important to them. The history and religion of Israel is dominated by the concept of nation. God was concerned not with individuals but with the black nation Israel. God supported the efforts of the black nation Israel. The black nation Israel made up the chosen people of God. God had a relationship with the nation Israel, and the nation Israel was to be saved or the nation Israel was to be punished. God spoke to a prophet that he might bring a message to the nation Israel. It is this concept of nation which Christianity loses entirely because of the apostle Paul's identification with the pagan white world. Black people of the nation Israel depended upon God to support them in every struggle. The Old Testament is a Black Power document that no modern book can equal. God would even hold the sun still while the black nation Israel killed its enemies. God would do anything necessary to help the black nation Israel find the promised land and keep it.

Jesus the black Messiah, lived in the midst of this kind of black liberation struggle. The Maccabean revolt freed Israel from white gentile oppression for a period, but by the time of Jesus, the Jews had again become an enslaved people who had lost much of their sense of nationhood. Jesus was born into a situation comparable to that in which black people in America live today. A situation in which black people were oppressed by a white gentile oppressor and were exploited in every way possible. Jesus found an underground revolutionary movement led by the Zealot extremists. The baptism of Jesus obviously marked his introduction into this revolutionary Zealot movement. When John the Baptist was arrested and about to be killed he sent disciples to talk to Jesus to find out whether or not he was the new leader who was to take over the movement. The terse reply of Jesus indicated quite clearly that he considered himself to be the new leader and that he was willing to be judged in terms of the things he was doing. Tell John and let him decide whether or not I am the Messiah. Following the death of John the Baptist, Jesus became the visible head of the revolutionary Zealot movement. Certain radical phases of the movement remained underground and certainly Jesus was forced to walk a tightrope in his relationships with an oppressed people who were fighting for liberation by any means necessary, and those who were in collaboration with the white oppressors and who expected certain benefits from this relationship. It is this kind of situation which is revealed in the little incident in which Jesus is asked about paying taxes to Caesar. The revolutionaries advocated paying no taxes to Caesar. They argued that this was one way of ending oppression. Jesus could have replied, "No, don't pay taxes to Caesar"; that would have been a popular answer and would have satisfied the movement, but would have led to his immediate arrest by the government. Upon the other hand he could have said, "Pay taxes to Caesar." Then he would have alienated the movement and endangered his life, but Rome would have been satisfied. He said neither. He pointed to Caesar's picture on the coin and said, "Give unto Caesar the things that are Caesar's and unto God the things that are God's." This is the kind of double-talk that preachers still use whenever they do not consider a question really important.

One of the most confusing teachings of Jesus has to do with the love ethic which the apostle Paul attempted to universalize. Jesus was defining a tribal ethic for the black nation Israel. He was trying to bring together a people who were oppressed, and who had been fragmented by their oppression. Any oppressed people are filled with self-hate and tend to identify with their oppressors. Psychological studies of modern Jews in concentration camps under Hitler, indicate that the greater the oppression, the greater the identification. In concentration camps the Jews identified totally with their guards who exercized the power of life and death. They were not even permitted to take care of their bodily needs without the guard's permission. So the guard became for them a kind of God with whom they identified completely. This is true with any oppressed people. Jesus understood the many forces which separate an oppressed people from each other and make them betray brothers to serve the interests of their oppressors. So in dealing with his own people he had to talk much about love. And in this sense, many of the things that Jesus said sound remarkably like the things that I've heard Stokely Carmichael say in talking to a black group. Stokely Carmichael could come into a meeting jammed with thousands of people and his first reaction would be in terms of the people's relationships with one another. If there were brothers sitting down and sisters standing along the wall Stokely would ask the brothers to please get up and let the sisters have their seats, saying that a people must learn to respect their women. That might have sounded like hate to white people, but to black people it pointed out a whole new approach to the possibilities of black people living together. Most of his talk would be in terms of how black people must love each other and build whatever they were going to build in terms of new human relationships, which could protect black people from the white man's materialism and selfishness. Listening to Stokely, I understood the kind of thing that Jesus had to do to unite the black people of Israel. He had to talk to them about the transforming and redemptive power of love within the black nation. If a black brother strikes you upon one cheek turn to him the other cheek, because we must save every black brother for the nation if we are to survive. We can't say that this group of black people is not important or that group of black people is not important. Every black brother or sister has to be saved and brought into the black nation. This is what Jesus was talking about. Turn the other cheek, go the second mile, go a hundred miles if necessary, if in this way you can save a black brother. In the parable of the good Samaritan, Jesus is trying to make the same emphasis. The Samaritans were Jews. They were a lost tribe, despised because they rejected the temple in Jerusalem. Jesus said, this, too, is part of the Jewish nation and it must be saved.

Jews could no longer look down on any part of the black nation. The parable of the good Samaritan was merely an effort to show Israel that these people could no longer be despised. Jesus said it straight out when the brother came and asked what he ought to do if a brother refused to treat him properly. Jesus said, "Take another brother and go and talk to him. If he still refuses to do right take another brother and talk to him again. If he still refuses, put him out of the nation and treat him like a gentile." We try to forget that Jesus talked about white gentiles in this way. Put him outside the nation. Treat him like a gentile. If Jesus had been preaching universal love when he said, "Go the second mile" and "Turn the other cheek" he would not possibly have understood that the black nation Israel was separate and apart from its white gentile enemies. Jesus made the same point with the gentile woman who came to have her daughter healed. Jesus explained that he had come to the house of Israel. She replied that a rich man throws crumbs from the table to feed the dogs. Jesus healed the child, but not out of love or concern for the white gentile. Jesus had come to the nation Israel. He tried to build the nation Israel. He labored to bring together a people who could stand against their oppressors.

We could say that this doesn't sound very revolutionary. He engaged in little physical combat except in the almost symbolic act of driving the money changers out of the temple. He didn't shoot a gun, he didn't use a sword. Even in Gethsemane when the soldiers came to arrest him and Peter drew his sword, Jesus stopped him in a very practical way. A battle would have been futile. The disciples were neither equipped nor trained for battle. If he had planned to fight, Jesus would have been putting together an army all the way to Jerusalem. But to turn what he had been trying to do for the nation into a military struggle at the last moment would have been ridiculous. Jesus was primarily concerned with building a people, bringing them together, and forming a nation. And this task to which Jesus gave his full commitment is profoundly revolutionary. Everything that Jesus taught, everything that he said is relevant to the liberation struggle in which black people are engaged. Instead of telling black people about escaping from the world and going home to God on high, the black church must begin to involve black people in the black liberation struggle, using the teachings of Jesus in the Synoptic Gospels, and the Old Testament concept of nation to show black people how coming together with black pride and Black Power is basic to survival. The black church must become central in the black revolution. Jesus was a black Messiah not in terms of his death on Calvary, but in terms of his dedication to the struggle of black people here on earth. In the black church the sacraments can take on a new meaning. At the Shrine of the Black Madonna we baptize into the nation. We die to the old Uncle Tom life. We die to the old identification with white people. To be baptized into a black church must symbolize a complete rejection of the values of a hostile white world and a complete commitment to the struggle of black people. When we take the sacrament of Holy Communion it symbolizes our total rededication to personal participation in the struggle of black people and total rededication to the black nation. The sacraments and ritual of the church then become for black people an intrinsic part of the revolutionary struggle.

Since all the great religions of the world derive from the black experience, we could turn to another religion if we wished. They all belong to us. Or we could put together a new religion suitable to our present needs and true to our historic revelations of God. But for black people in America, Christianity is part of our past. Its reinterpretation in terms of its historic black roots is a joyful task which we have undertaken. To finally realize that Jesus is a black Messiah, that the things he taught are still relevant to us, and that the distortions which we have learned are deliberate distortions perpetrated by the white man for his own benefit and convenience, is to realize that the restoration of the original Christianity taught by Jesus, is a task which we cannot put aside. We can restructure theology, making it something that black people can understand and appreciate. In many places young black people are honestly ashamed to be seen going in or coming out of a church. Understandably so because the black church has been an Uncle Tom institution, committed to the preservation of the white status quo and the pacification of black people. A revolutionary black church must be a place to which black people come with pride, knowing that Jesus was black, that the nation Israel was black, and that we are following in the footsteps of a black Messiah. Even now we are restructuring the black church that it may become the foundation upon which we build the black Christian nationalist liberation struggle and the emerging black nation.

# Chapter Two

# HOW BLACK IS BLACK RELIGION?

*Joseph R. Washington, Jr.*

A decade or so ago, Will Herberg wrote the classic *Protestant, Catholic, Jew*. In it he successfully demonstrated America to be a transmuting pot in which immigrants from diverse heritages found it imperative to shed their culture, including language and nationality, in order to participate fully in the American mainstream. To be an American mainliner means that one can identify with one's past, and thereby find one's identity, only as a Protestant, Catholic, Jew, or Eastern Orthodox, and then only to the extent the religious heritage is transmuted into the "American way of life."

As far as Blacks are concerned, Herberg made clear they are excluded from the mainstream. The black man is not accepted as a Protestant, Catholic, Jew, or an Eastern Orthodox, as is a white man, and he cannot find his identity therein as do other Americans. Blacks are like other Americans in that it has been unacceptable for them to identify with their past culture in Africa, but they are unlike other Americans in that the loss of a past cultural identity was neither voluntarily given up nor provided a substitute by way of becoming a mainliner.

This double jeopardy, double damnation, had been largely accepted as inevitable by scholars like Will Herberg and mainstream America, until the recent emergence of militant Blacks who not only dare to defy the American way of life by nurturing the African past as a competitive culture, but who also claim they do not wish to become mainliners—injecting into their veins the deadly poison of white America. White America reacts as if it has been deeply wronged and wounded when the people it has ruled out of bounds draws upon a resource which purports to leave them out, when white America is not expressing disbelief. There are a few liberals who now say it is acceptable for the old pluralism of Protestant, Catholic, and Jew to give way to a new pluralism of Protestant, Catholic, Jew, and Black. This verbal reversal or concession is made on the grounds that Blacks cannot pull it off and if they can pull it off it is preferable to a radical disruption of society and its structures.

The only "status" Blacks have had in America was in slavery. It is against the American faith for Blacks to gain status in America apart from the shackles of slavery. It is against the grain of the American way of life for Blacks to realize their identity and accept it and transform it into assets, for it is viewed, if at all, as a liability. Negative responses to black rhetoric about black reality and black experience and black perspective and Black Power are only symptomatic. The real source of white reaction to black pride and black consciousness is the myth that refuses to be demythologized. More than a quarter of a century ago, Melville J. Herskovits, writing in *The Myth of the Negro Past,* lampooned the great American myth that "the Negro is a man without a past." Old myths do not die, they simply become dysfunctional or meaningless, when not demythologized, in the new reality structured by different values and norms and attitudes and experiences and actions.

Of all people, scholars in religious studies should have been the first to dismiss this American myth. Instead, scholars in religion have chosen to accept the hypotheses and speculations and generalizations and theories of social scientists, especially anthropologists. But is it any wonder? The scholars of religion accept the American way of life, at least insofar as it applies to the black man. Perhaps this is the real reason why they have failed to carry out their own research in this virgin field. In the midst of this vacuum, religious scholars have nothing with which to counter their colleagues in other disciplines.

Let us see if we can discover just how black black folk religion is and what it holds for the American myth that "the Negro is a man without a past."

Indentured Blacks came to America in 1620, landing at Jamestown. The Blacks who came as slaves were Africans, the majority of whom were from West Africa. Obviously, the American slaves were ripped from the African culture, they were not just savages or animal property. The strangeness of the West African culture was excuse enough for the slave traders and masters to promote and perpetuate the myth that this strange culture was no culture.

Africans became acculturated slower in other slave centers of the New World. The African attitudes, customs, politics, social and economic systems, the technology of ironworking, woodcarving, weaving, and, of course, language, still is readily discernible in the rest of the Americas—Haiti, Brazil, Cuba, Guiana, for example—where gradations of pure African culture exist today.

It was the intimate association between Africans and the small farmers of the United States, who owned the vast majority of slaves, which led to the rapid acculturation here and the repression of African culture. Coupled with the pattern of intimate association, the general acculturation of Africans resulted from their ancient belief that the more powerful gods of other tribes were to be revered. These two factors combined with white America's insistence that everything African was not only inferior primitivism but had to be eliminated, on the pretense that throwing off the past would speed acceptance, advance the capitulation of Africans here to the dominant white mode or model.

Africans in general and West Africans in particular were rooted in a society highly determined by intense religion at all levels. This affirmation of the supernatural was one of the heritages which Africans found congenial in the new culture, although the rituals and patterns of worship had to be drastically changed. The reason syncretism—let alone African independent worship—did not become the form or response or the new black religion was that the white masters early perceived the worship of African gods through African rituals to be not only primitive but an effective instrument of escape, rebellion, and insurrection as well. Any reference to African gods or customs of worship was immediately squashed on pain of brutal beatings or death. If the *Pueblo's* Captain Bucher quickly sized up the situation and decided that a fight to the death of all his crew was not worth the principle of not fighting back, the slaves who were even more heavily outnumbered should not be thought of as without courage or culture if they chose uncertain life over certain death. Clearly the African's native drum was not allowed the slave because it was as readily adaptable for a call to escape or insurrection as a call to dance.

The point of all this is by way of questioning the claim of social scientists that every strand of the African culture was eliminated from the black man. Among the African impress which was not discharged from the black psyche was religion and its concomitants of music and dance. African culture did not distinguish between music, dance, song, rhythm, and worship of the gods. Through the medium of music, dance, song, on the beat of rhythm, religion survived the slave repression experience. The language and concepts were changed but the rhythmic beat of religious music and total outpouring through dance and song survived and can be found to this day in the churches of black folks. There is in black religion an aliveness, intensity of joy and ecstasy, which is infectious because it is uninhibited. In addition to the rhythmic beat, the religious service continues to be driven by antiphonal singing, as in African music, where the leader sings a lead line and it is answered by a congregation in chorus. Another important survival in the worship of black folk is the African dependency upon improvisation.

Earlier we indicated why the more impressive rites of African religion survived only in bits and pieces and then only through clandestine activities. But even today, if one searches hard enough, in isolated areas of the rural South, the mixture of voodoo and other African fetish religions with Christianity can be found.

Of course the special attraction which Baptists held for the slaves was their form of baptism via immersion. The precedent of Christ here was important later on, but at first the fact that most of the religions of West Africa held the river spirits to be the most powerful of the gods had a singular effect.

Insofar as Methodist and Baptist were the most popular religious forms for Africans, this appeal and response had to do with the emotionalism of their evangelism. There is an old African dictum that "the spirit will not descend without a song."

In African religious rituals emotional frenzies were a dynamic and integral part. Ritual dances and songs and emotional frenzies of African religious "total letting go" are among the lasting contributions to the religion of black folk in America. Black folk religion is highly charged with emotion to this day. "Spirit possession" of the African religions has become "getting religion" or "getting happy," so indispensable to southern rural and nonmiddle-class urban folk religion. Dancing in worship was frowned upon by the white culture, but it has persisted in the religious dances by the beat of drums and tambourines among the "holiness" or "sanctified" black religious folk. The influence of Blacks upon the more "sanctified" forms of worship among Whites is obvious. One hundred years ago, a typical black service of worship was described in the following manner:

> The benches were pushed back to the wall when the formal meeting is over, and old and young, men and women, sprucely dressed young men, grotesquely half-clad field hands —the women generally with gay handkerchiefs twisted about their heads and with short skirts—boys with tattered shirts and men's trousers, young girls bare-footed, all stand up in the middle of the floor, and when the "sperichil" is struck up begin walking and by and by shuffling around, one after another, in a ring. The foot is hardly taken from the floor, and the procession is mainly due to a jerking, hitching motion which agitates the entire shouter and soon brings out streams of perspiration. Sometimes they dance silently, sometimes as they shuffle they sing the chorus of the spiritual, and sometimes the song itself is also sung by the dancers. But more frequently a band, composed of the best singers and of tired shouters, stand at the side of the room to "base" the others, singing the body of the song and clapping their hands together or on the knees. Song and dance are alike extreme energetic, and often, when the shout lasts into the middle of the night, the monotonous thud, thud of feet prevents sleep within half a mile of the praise house.[1]

Religion was the center for dance, music, and song among black folk, as well as politics, drama, community, self-expression, and self-identification. It is true, music or drama or dance or poetry or community or politics are now, to a very large extent, black forces independent of black folk religion. It is also true that black folk religion is still dependent upon these forces for its life and power and uniqueness.

[1] H. E. Krehbid, *The Nation*, May 30, 1867.

Black folk religion created music of pure African heritage which was changed in response to the American restrictions. Nowhere is the African melody clearer than in the spirituals whose words were changed to fit the English language and experience and biblical teachings. The Bible taught that the Jews were an oppressed people and this Christian scripture made its impact upon suffering Blacks. The spirituals are the remnant of this legacy, the yearning for freedom and justice and equality and the "Promised Land."

The development of black folk religion in America cannot be understood apart from the singular role of African music, a fact that was true as well of African religion. We see this in the spirituals, the sources of which were the African rhythm together with the Bible, nature, and personal experiences and hopes. Here the identification in suffering with the Jews and especially with Jesus is unmistakable. Without elaborating upon this theme, it is well to point out that the importance of music in the religion of Blacks as inherited from Africa is further evidenced in the singular role of the black preacher.

The black preacher made superb use of African folktales, parables, riddles, proverbs, which were increasingly left behind for biblical stories and the American slave experience, for the chief method of education in African culture was the wisdom of the elders thereby passed on to the young. Not only was the black preacher a superb artist in telling a story, his dramatic presentations were more often than not accented by his musical leadership in the most emotional parts of the sermon or story. Sermons were rhythmical, sometimes sung in parts to gain that added feeling and emphasis. The power of this verbal-rhythmic combination in song was a continuation in a new mode of the ancient African tradition of call-and-response or participation by all the gathered, which the music of Africa demands. The chants, hollers, shouts in rhythmic syncopation and shifted accents with vibrato all were African in form if not in content. The key to the black preacher was his ability to so dramatize the sermon that the people were pulled into a direct response. His slow beginning, studdering out at key points for dramatic effect so that the people would feel forced to say it for him, the repetition—all are demonstrated in black folk services. Such a

service might take off with the spiritual "'Have you got religion?' Certainly, Lord!" When a black preacher and congregation are in tune their music and rhythm are pure African and
pure beauty. There is nothing comparable in religion to the
black preacher and congregation in rhythmic call and response:

> We are an enslaved race, cut off from our past and at the
> mercy of our present. (Amen.) But our Lord has spoken to
> Pharaoh's heart through a prophet: "Let my people go, that
> they may serve me." (Amen, Amen.) We have endured hard
> trials! (Yes, Lord, yes, Lord.) They seem to be getting worse.
> (Worse, Lord, worse!) Do you believe the Lord will deliver us?
> (Yes, he will; yes, he will.) Have you ever doubted it? (No,
> never doubted it.) He will make a way out of no way. (My,
> my, my.) The Lord is our strength and song, our salvation.
> (Go right on, don't stop now!) "I sing because I'm happy. I
> sing because I'm free. His eye is on the sparrow, and I know he
> watches me." (Yes he does! Amen, brother, preach, preach.)

The point has been made. The American myth that "the
Negro is a man without a past" does not hold water when the
religion of black folks is seriously studied. Of course the full
evidence cannot be set forth in a short paper, but perhaps there
are suggestions enough for fruitful exploration. If we were to
focus on the wider aspects we could see how blues and jazz and
dance were initially formulated in the black church and rooted
in Africa. Here it is enough to point up how black folk religion
is rooted in Africa and how Africa is rooted in black religion.
In the beginning was the black church, and the black church
was with the black community, and the black church was the
black community. The black church was in the beginning with
the black people; all things were made through the black
church, and without the black church was not anything made
that was made. In the black church was life, and the life was
the light of the black people. The black church still shines in
the darkness, and the darkness has not overcome it.

Arnold Toynbee is the best example of the typical social
scientist and religionist in his deprecation of the black man's
resources before the 1620 Jamestown landing:

> The Negro has not, indeed, brought any ancestral religion
> of his own from Africa to captivate the hearts of his White
> fellow-citizens in America. His primitive social heritage was of
> so frail a texture that, save for a few shreds, it was scattered
> to the winds on the impact of our Western Civilization. Thus
> he came to America spiritually as well as physically naked; and

*

he has met with the emergency by covering his nakedness with
his enslaver's cast-off clothes.[2]
This misinterpretation of history in praise of Western civilization, without batting an eyelash vis-à-vis its concentration camp
tactics, and in damnation of African culture, would be tragic
were it not so blatantly erroneous. Given what we have all too
briefly suggested in the preceding paragraphs, Toynbee has to
be taken with a bushel of salt. He is right in what he affirms,
but wrong in what he denies.

Actually, Toynbee is dangerous because he means well.
He damns the black man with feigned praise as engaged in
wishful thinking, rather than in scholarship. In the following
passage, a continuation of the above quotation, Toynbee prays
for white folks and preys upon black folks as he views the root
of black religion from the white rather than from the black
experience:

> The Negro has adapted himself to his new social environ-
> ment by rediscovering in Christianity certain original mean-
> ings and values which Western Civilization has long ignored.
> Opening a simple and impressionable mind to the Gospels, he
> has discovered that Jesus was a prophet who came into the
> world not to confirm the mighty in their seats but to exalt the
> humble and meek. The Syrian slave immigrants who once
> brought Christianity into Roman Italy performed the miracle
> of establishing a new religion which was alive in the place of
> an old religion which was already dead. It is possible that the
> Negro slave immigrants who have found Christianity in Amer-
> ica may perform the greater miracle of raising the dead to
> life. With their childlike spiritual intuition and their genius
> for giving spontaneous aesthetic expression to emotional reli-
> gious experience, they may perhaps be capable of kindling the
> cold gray ashes of Christianity which have been transmitted to
> them by us until, in their hearts, the divine fire flows again.
> It is thus, perhaps, if at all, that Christianity may conceivably
> become the living faith of a dying civilization for the second
> time. If this miracle were indeed to be performed by an Ameri-
> can Negro Church, that would be the most dynamic response
> to the challenge of social penalization that had yet been made
> by man.[3]

Toynbee ignores the fact that black people are about doing their
own thing in a thoroughly repressive society, together with the
fact that the majority of Blacks have never been Christians.

---

[2] Arnold Toynbee, *A Study of History*, abr. by D. C. Somervill (New
York: Oxford University Press, 1947), p. 129.
[3] Ibid.

To look to the downtrodden and oppressed to redeem a dying civilization and a dying Christianity is an extraordinary hope based on fear, for the contribution of black folks may be by way of death and rebirth; rather than resuscitation we would do well to look to resurrection.

So, the myth persists about the past of the black man, his culture and therefore religion. Even more important today is the modernist revision of this myth which holds that the black man has no culture of any consequence. Some social scientists will concede that the rural folk religion of southern Blacks had some cultural strands, but, that is past and today Blacks are discoverable only in sociological statistics: poverty, fear, unemployment, rape, mayhem, mugging, ill-housing, ill-health, illegitimacy, desertion, and welfare payments. The modern version of the black man without a past is that of the black man without a present, without a culture or religion or identity.

We have suggested that the blackness of black religion is to be found rooted in the culture of Africa past. Let us see if the flower of this root is discoverable today, if, indeed, the black man is without religion and culture.

Some years ago, two scholars who have subsequently gained national recognition, Nathan Glazer and Daniel Moynihan, wrote a book entitled *Beyond the Melting Pot* in which they asserted that "the Negro is only an American and nothing else. He has no values and culture to guard and protect." Writing in *The Mark of Oppression,* Abram Kardiner and Lionel Ovesey stated: "We have seen little evidence of genuine religiosity among Negroes. They have invented no religion of their own." In *Crisis in Black and White,* Charles Silberman continued this revisionism: "In contrast to European immigrants, who brought rich cultures and long histories with them, the Negro has been completely stripped of his past and severed from any culture save that of the United States."

We need only to recall Will Herberg's thesis to refute the assumption that the black man is the most American of Americans from the point of view of dominant Whites, who count, but, it is necessary to look at the black man as a black man to refute the assumption, from his perspective, that he brought nothing into this society and builds on nothing of his own in the present. We have held forth that the black man is a man with a past. It is now necessary to hold forth that the black man is a man with a culture which he needs to accept and transform into a vital force for his own humanity. The fact is, as we shall suggest, the black man has done a great deal for himself. His failures are the best proof of his successes.

The root of black folk religion in African rhythm, music, dance, and participating sermons has flowered among Blacks in the rural South and urban ghettos as frenzied dancing, tambourine-playing, speaking in tongues, screaming sermons, instrumental groups, hand-clapping, and total congregational participation in worship. Black folk religion today is to be found among the masses as has always been the case, for they are the bulk of black people and they are the black folk. The man in the street, on *Tally's Corner*, knows a religion that is the key to black folk religion.

The man in the street who claims that "the white man's heaven is the black man's hell" may not lead one directly to the flowering of black folk religion today, but he will indirectly.

Black culture has its special domain in black folk religion, the locus where black people have proved and preserved their identity. Black folk religion is experiential first and foremost. It begins and ends in the experience of the black folk. It is a religion of acting out or dramatizing the experience of the people through uninhibited feeling expressed in powerful tones. It was rooted in Africa, transplanted in slavery, nurtured in segregation, developed in discrimination, and flowered in integration. Black folk religion follows the life style of Blacks and takes on the color and form necessary to meet the oppression dominant at a given historical point in the American experience.

The religion of black folk is a religion of ritual, drama, and "dialectical catharsis." The key to black folk religion is the power with which the black unconscious is stirred through ritualization. This religion of ritual power is not limited to churches or the sacred; it is best perceived as a real blend of the sacred and secular—that's where black religion is, for that is where life is. Those who possess this ritual power are black preachers, disc jockeys, singers, musicians, hustlers, comedians, and athletes. These ritualists are in the long line of black ritualists, they have "soul power" because they have tapped the "soul tradition" at its African roots.

Ritualistic performances or entertainment make up only one strand in the black culture, but the most visible strand for the novice. There are four basic aspects of this strand in black culture: (1) it is rooted in West Africa and these rituals were not eliminated by slavery; (2) the ritual strand has not only survived but increased amidst suffering; (3) the ritual tradition is immediately accessible to anyone who is sensitive to black music, songs, dance, and rhetoric; and (4) black ritualists are masters of rhythm, timing, improvisation, verbal expression, sound, and movement.

It is the shared sensibilities of black folk that one must participate in to uncover black culture, not just the written documents of middle-class Blacks who alone write or the institutions and structures they pattern after the white folk. The aural-oral qualities speak of black culture and provide the clear channel of expressive communication among black folk.

Perhaps it can no longer be claimed that the black preacher is the foremost ritualist of the black community. Yet, when the black preacher is really a turned-on man he still is to be reckoned with as a culture hero of the black folk. The key to the black culture hero is that he be able to entertain, be clever, and possess the capacity to be economically well off without having to grind it out for a living. The preacher is rivaled today by the hustler, the comedian, the athlete, the singer, and the musician as the culture hero of the black folk. But the point is that the black folk look to these black ritualists as heroes, and, the hero is always the much berated black male, not the black woman. The black preacher may be losing ground, but he is still a potent hero among black women, who, after all, are the supporters of the congregation.

The flowering of black folk religion may best be seen in West African rhythm in fusion with European harmony. Black music is composed of blues and jazz, spirituals, jubilees, and gospels. The fusion today of blues, jazz, and gospel music into what we know as "soul music" is a special instance of the integration of church and secular dimensions of black folk religion. Soul music is a music of the soul of the masses, the black folk.

Black culture has emerged from the black experience into a black reality. This black reality or expression or experience is unmistakable among Blacks in their dance, religion, music, drama, and slang which has penetrated beyond black people into the life of white people.

It is not by accident that our exploration into the flowering of black folk religion takes the form of discussing "soul." "Soul," the communication of the black experience, which forges the black reality, took root in the earliest religious experiences of black folk. The black church served black folk as the matrix for its life in the past, it is nonetheless so today with soul music. This center of black folk which gave shape to the black experience and structured the black reality, the black church, is no longer the dominant, all-embracing, or cerebral center of the black community. Yet, the black culture or experience cannot be grasped—or better still, you cannot be grasped by the black culture or experience—apart from coming to terms with the black church.

It is obvious that many blues and "soul singers" began their careers in gospel choirs; some become, in time, preachers or gospel singers or both. The battle of gospel choirs is not different in style and tone from that of "soul groups," which leads one to suggest the radical possibilities of black music, especially soul music, vis-à-vis the unity of black masses. Black music is subversive; it has power of revolutionary dimensions, as well as a means of conversion. The gospel music, blues, and jazz are so intertwined that few blues singers today or soul singers, have not made their way to the top via a church choir. The number of storefront churches with gospel choirs gives pause for reflection, let alone the impact of gospel music on blues and jazz and white America via techtronics.

It is in these strands of black culture that one sees the flowering of black folk religion. The close relationship between the styles of singing and preaching among blues singers and gospel ministers indicates the interchangeability of their roles —they each preach or moralize to the black community, only different parts of it, with nearly identical messages. It may be that black religion has flowered to the point where it is more dependent upon soul music for its special way of worshiping than soul music is dependent upon black religion. Yet, it would be foolhardy to sell black religion in the churches short. The words of the Supremes may differ from those of the gospel singers in the churches, but the beat and rhythm and message is the same, for the medium is the message and the message of soul is the medium. Aretha Franklin, "Lady Soul," daughter of the Rev. C. L. Franklin of Detroit, is the best example of the pervasive influence of the black church in the sphere of soul music. Whether or not her father is the flowering of black folk religion via his chanted parables and repetitious sermonic phrases is at best an open question.

The way into the black culture and experience is through black folk religion, the alpha and omega of the black reality. It must be reiterated that the flowering of black folk religion cannot be by way of dwelling on the black church because the black community does do so. The black community has taken the experience formed in black churches and advanced it in various black media. We must, however, identify the black church's strand in the flowering of black religion for there we are sure of being on the track of the black experience and the black reality—a significant strand in the black culture. In black churches is found soul. There is no way to soul; soul is the way.

This may not be the age of miracles, but it is rather miraculous that the concept of soul which has lost all meaning and relevance for white American culture is such a dynamic and powerful expression of those who are said to be without culture —the black masses. Indeed, soul has become contagious to the point of being infectious. Soul unites Blacks on the left and on the right, whether they be Black Muslims or black integrationists or black nationalists or Black Power—Blacks have soul. The concept of soul is not devoid of religious meaning in even its more nonreligious expressions. There is a soul of black folk that is indomitable; it is the root and flower of black folk religion.

There is blackness in black folk religion. It is rooted. It has flowered. Will it now dry up and wither away? Some believe its resources are so deep as to make black religion an eternal spring. Yet, the source of such optimism is the assumption that the blackness of black religion can and should be measured only by its emotional and ritualistic power. No doubt this past contribution merits appreciation, but it is not enough to meet the needs of black people today. Black religion is more bleak than black to the extent it is not injected with depth of knowledge and understanding to engage the present by the future beyond the past.

We are in a transitional period in human history. The era which began with the Renaissance ended with the advent of World War I. This time between the times is one in which the myths and symbols of the era past are powerless. Ours is a time of frustration, confusion, and uncertain direction. When one historical period ends it is to be expected that problems will become dominant over solutions, conflict over progress, disengagement over unity. Especially is this the case when a people are internally torn by a fundamental issue.

With respect to this issue, black Americans are in a worse position than five years ago. For black Americans particularly, the old patterns and slogans and myths and truisms are deadly and dying.

The death of the old order provides opportunity for the birth of a new order with new myths and new symbols. Myths and symbols provide direction and meaning and purpose and hope which men cannot live significantly without, nor can they create them at will. The only way to recognize a myth is by the power which emanates from it.

One new myth breaking forth out of the new age breaking in is Black Power. The power of this myth for black people in particular and all people in general is everywhere in evidence. To be sure, Black Power has yet fully to emerge as a myth. But it is the one sure myth of the future, the future of black people.

Black Power is a movement of, from, and for black people. Black Power is in the best interest of black people and thus the best interest of all people. Black Power is the future of black people. It is also the future of black religion. Since Black Power and black people are inextricably intertwined, the future of the black church and thus black religion is in relation to its support of Black Power or black people.

The task of the black church among black people is to meet their needs, to support and advance that which is in the real interest of black people. If the black church is to make a contribution to black people it will not be by way of turning black people or Black Power around it as the center or leader. To contribute, the black church must develop a theology of Black Power or black people.

Defenders of the black church qua black church believe there is something unique in this colorful sphere which transcends the standards of doctrine, discipline, and worship that may determine the peculiarities of each religious body lumped under this umbrella called the black church. Black congregations and denominations may be free, integral, and independent parts of the church of Christ, but if one were to ask of the clergy and laymen engaged in black religious institutions to enumerate their distinctive teachings they would be hard put to indicate their contributions to American churchianity.

It is important to make clear that divisions among religious bodies are not in themselves without merit or value. It may be held that the divisions of black institutions which are but colored reproductions of white institutions, with a difference in emphasis, have potential richness for all men. Can unity of black Christians come about through the separation of Blacks in different black institutions? That is, is not the question confronting black Christians one of a unity of Blacks for encounter first with white Christians in our society, second with all men and women in our society, third with men and women of other world religions, and fourth with men and women throughout the world? The point I wish to make is that given these various levels of understanding and confrontation, precious little thinking has been done on the part of black laymen and clergymen.

To be quite candid, given Black Power and the conditions for its emergence, it is a little late in the day to be concerned about the particularities and peculiarities of black religion vis-à-vis white denominations as regards issues of doctrine, discipline, and worship. The future in and the future of black churches is in the area of theology rather than doctrine, in the area of community rather than discipline, and in the area of action rather than worship. In theology, community, and action the black church may find its unity in Black Power to confront the world in general and the Christian community in particular so as to give black people direction. Insofar as the black church loses its life there is some hope that we may yet all gain life.

The future in and the future of black churches is dependent upon its clarification with regard to its intentions, its purposes, and its objectives or goals. This calls for theological understanding and conviction and commitment and lucidity. Given the dynamic leadership of Black Power, what else besides theology can the black church contribute? It is time for the black church to be a thinking church, for to be a moral force requires thought in action. What does it mean for the black church to be the people of God in the twentieth century? Does this call for a change with respect to specifics in the life of worship, in the actions of the religious community in the larger community? To glorify God in the midst of brokenness, violence, and revolution demands deeds beyond words for the reconstruction of humanity. The Christian cannot engage in such glorification of God apart from theological sharpness, creative insight, and innovative imagination by black people in black places with black opportunities confronting obstruction. The preciseness and specific knowledge in action is the work of a whole people combining the variety of their skills and wisdom and knowledge in persuasive power to enlighten themselves and their community through which the gospel shines forth in relevant deeds in the community.

The future in the black church depends upon this kind of interior moral knowledge and action in every congregation, community, and denomination. What are the problems in each community, what are black churchmen to do in each community if they are to glorify God and uplift man?

Are black churchmen about a knowledge and an action in their community which is different from that of other churchmen? Are black churchmen called to further divide men in order that real unity or reconciliation can come forth? Can there be any real life of the church, any real soul, without the life of the mind? Where there is no mind there is no church and there is no soul.

The black church is called to be not only a reflective and action-initiated community of those whose will and purpose is to glorify God and uplift man in thought and deed, but also to be the community which puts to work its institutional power in support of its moral thought and action. Do black churches have institutional power and authority? If they have, it is by and large squandered without any real serious economic, political, and social impact. It is incumbent upon the black church to discover what its ministry, indeed, its special ministry has to be. When this discovery has been made then it is incumbent upon the black church to see that that ministry takes place wherever black people are. Institutional life needs to be concerned about black people in large urban areas, suburban areas, small towns, and villages. It needs to be concerned about affluent and poverty-stricken Blacks, status-seeking and status-denied Blacks, middle-class and middle-class-aspiring Blacks, Blacks who attend church and those who do not. To make any kind of an impact upon Blacks throughout the community at all levels will require institutional power as well as moral discernment, but an institutional power that is efficiently mobilized and directed.

If the critical thinking or theology in the black churches has been historically weak, institutional efficiency has been even more of a waste. One need but look at financial distribution of resources that Blacks have, the development and distribution of church school materials, the education of ministers and laymen, to name but a few.

An example of the lack of institutional efficiency may be permitted here. When I was a grade-school youngster growing up in a small midwestern town the presiding elder of the African Methodist Episcopal Church was an impressive and handsome gentleman from Chicago. He was loved by all the members of that community who belonged to that church, and I have every reason to believe this was true throughout his district. This past summer I was asked to lecture before the ministers of that district at one of their camp retreats. I discovered that the gentleman who was the presiding elder when I was a child continues to be a presiding elder. He is now in his late 70's or early 80's, nearly blind, and totally dependent upon others to do his work.

There is no doubt in my mind but that to make the institutions of the black church efficient is a fantastic job, almost beyond what seems feasible. Yet, if the black church is to be an independent institution to meet the needs of black people it cannot do so without beginning now to reshape its institutional life. Frankly, I do not know just how this is to be done. I only know that the future in and the future of black churches is dependent upon clarity of thought, efficiency of institutional power, vitality of self-criticism, and a vision toward which its initiating activity moves in creative ways amidst Black Power.

I take it that a call to consultation on the black church is an attempt to unify black people in spirit and purpose beyond their conflicting religious emphases and cultic practices. It is true, uniqueness may be difficult to determine as regards the doctrines and disciplines of the various black sects and denominations, but their faith and life, preaching and teaching have had an extraordinary impact upon the morals of black people, if not upon their politics. Black religion has been a definite factor in giving shape to the life of black people and therefore to the nation, though this may not be precisely identified.

It is the theology of freedom, however, which I perceive to be the special province of the black church, a theology which has not been developed commensurate with the black experience. It is obvious that the very life of black people has been one concerned with freedom and that the very life of the church has been one concerned with dogmatism, arbitrariness, authoritarianism, and coercion. Black people are all concerned about their freedom and thus they are concerned with freedom as a humanizing power. Freedom as a humanizing dimension is the very substance of black people which does not need to be searched out in some obscure and special methodology; it is present in the hunger and thirst of the people. The hunger for freedom may not be realized through black churches if they continue to place their emphasis upon self-interest, tradition, narrow loyalties, ambition, status, security, and the quest for recognition.

Given the American pattern of churchianity, black churches have every right to exist. But with rights come responsibilities. The particular responsibility of black churches is to contribute to the needs of black people and therefore to the

society as a whole. In fact, black churches have no other responsibility than to contribute to the freedom of black people.
Richard Allen and the other founding fathers of the black
church expected that these institutions would promote freedom
among black people and let it ring throughout the nation. Black
people are of the same mind today and it would be bad faith
for black churches not to act upon this faith in the present.

The time has come to be clear about the fact that the task
of the church is to promote the well-being of humanity, the
only way humanity can glorify God. The well-being of man cannot exist apart from freedom and therefore the task of the
church is to promote freedom. In this respect, black churches
do not hold any special kind of freedom vis-à-vis the supernatural versus the natural, or the public versus private. There
cannot be religious and secular freedom any more than there
can be religious and secular man. The question for the black
church is whether or not in the pursuit of freedom for black
people the black church has anything special to contribute. Is
there anything in the black church which can add to the depth
and lucidity of the idea of freedom among black people? Even
more important, to this date the black church has not developed
a theology, the critical and thinking dimension of religion. The
question is whether freedom as the fundamental concern of
black people, who of all people lack freedom the most, can be
the spur for the formation of a theology of black churches based
upon this common concern of freedom. It is my conviction that
freedom is the heart and whole of the black church, the essence
of the black church is freedom. The ultimate loyalty of the black
church is to the Lord of history. The test of the quality of
black existence is freedom. Without freedom black people will
perish and with them their neighbors. Only by the increase of
freedom among black people is there an opportunity for dynamic
peace open in the future. In a word, if one wishes to talk about
salvation, the only salvation the black church has to offer is
through freedom, the only hope of mankind. Freedom is the
religion of black people and the responsibility of churchmen to
increase it as the appropriate response to the Lord of history and
before all mankind.

Critical thinking in the black church or theology is the rethinking of what these communities mean vis-à-vis the religion of freedom. Black people need more than anything else to look again at what freedom has meant in their history and what it means in their present. Freedom is the essence of black religion and therefore the unifying principle of faith and life among black people in which it is the task of a black theology of freedom to illuminate. There is only freedom; it is not to be opposed by spiritual or moral or political or economic or secular or humanistic freedom. It is only through searching into the history and meaning of black people in the light of freedom and bringing to bear this theology or critical thinking upon the present that a contribution is made to black people and thus to all people by the black church under the aegis of Black Power.

There are those who may question whether or not the black church has anything to contribute with regard to the issue of freedom. If it does not, then it has nothing to contribute with respect to any issue.

The significance of a theology of freedom has to be seen in the context of the larger secular development of Black Power. This merits repetition because the power of Black Power is crucial! We are at the end of an age, in the beginning of a new one. The old symbols and myths are dead or dying rapidly. New symbols and new myths are necessary to bring us into the new age. The only way to tell whether or not a myth is significant is by the power which breaks forth from it. One new myth that is breaking forth with power is the myth of Black Power. It needs to be increased via innovation and imagination. An authentic black theology of freedom would begin with its response to God and to its fellowmen through an engagement in intellectual combat with Black Power as to the nature of the freedom pursued by all in behalf of all.

Freedom is to be the central theological task of the black church because it is the central thrust of black people. The life of freedom needs to be the life of the black church. This theology is not to be a substitute for Black Power but out of its biblical theology it is to be an effort toward unlocking the biblical tradition and its meaning in the present on behalf of black people or Black Power.

It may be the case that black people have not been unique

as churchmen in their opposition to thinking, but even the professionals in the black church have not, until recently, been thinking or critical, or theologians. The time is past when we can be concerned about just raising professional theologians. We need to work out a black theology by black people who are laymen as well as clergymen. Faith and freedom are interwoven and black people must know how faith and freedom are indispensable dimensions each to the other.

With the development of Black Power and the world in which black people live, it is imperative that black people think in terms of how in the midst of Black Power a contribution can be made to God without violating faith or freedom. In the life of faith and worship the central response is to God and as the people gather together it is creative and real only insofar as the gathering is free.

Up to this point, there have been ideas which black churchmen and the black church contributed to black people which have been countered by their divisiveness and competitiveness which has resulted in the failure to foster unity among black people. If there is to be unity among black people there must be freedom; freedom and unity are indispensable to black people. Unless the black church is engaged in developing a theology of freedom on a foundation of unity there will be no significant contribution which the black church can make to black people or Black Power.

It needs to be made clear that the only real force which demands that black people develop a theology of freedom is Black Power. Black Power is a new force for a new age which is an emerging myth that places pressure upon the churches. It does not matter whether or not advocates of Black Power who are not advocates of the black church agree with black churchmen and their development of a black theology of freedom. What does matter is that all understand that the question of freedom is not a question of intellectual abstraction but of the necessity of black people; whether they be Christians or no is quite beside the point. Black theologians must engage in the question of freedom to increase the stature of black people.

Finally, beyond the theology of freedom the future in and the future of black churches is in the development of the theology of suffering. I have made some suggestions toward developing a theology of suffering in my work *The Politics of God*. This needs to be refined and developed, but this understanding of suffering against the background of an understanding of freedom helps to give black people a sense of who they are in the midst of Black Power and the world confronted thereby. Beyond the theology of freedom and the theology of suffering there must be developed a theology of revolution. It just may be that all our efforts to the contrary, revolution may come about. If revolution comes about, it needs to be intelligent, it needs to have direction, and it needs to be of the people. If a revolution emerges that is intelligent, innovative, positive, and of the people, the black church will not be able to sit by and say we are for black people but against revolution. This is the test of the blackness of black religion. How black is black religion? We can answer this only by the future of the black church in its theological participation in the future of Black Power, which is the future of black people.

# Chapter Three

# THE GOD-CONSCIOUSNESS OF THE BLACK CHURCH IN HISTORICAL PERSPECTIVE

*Walter L. Yates*

In February, when I was invited by the Rev. Mr. James J. Gardiner, to share in the Conference on Black Church/Black Theology I was most enthusiastic. But as I started to narrow the scope and to consider my share of the responsibility—the God-consciousness of the black church in historical perspective—my spirits subsided and my enthusiasm went on vacation.

The present investigation is limited to those aspects of the religious history that are more or less related directly or indirectly to the black or darker ethnic branches of the human family, and their religion and culture. I agree with C. Loring Brace when he says:

> Culture, includes not only the high points of art, music, and literature, but also all those things that result from cumulative efforts of other people and previous generations. Tools, the traditions regulating their use, vital information, and language itself, all are included in the concept of culture. Man is not just an animal that possesses culture, but an animal that cannot survive without it. . . .
>
> In the beginning our ancestors, like other animals, must have been faced with the problem of surviving without the aid of culture. So much of culture is perishable or intangible that there is no way to determine when culture as a cumulative phenomenon began. Nonperishable cultural elements have an antiquity of about two million years in Africa. The culture tradition of which they are a part continues without break, expanding to occupy the tropical and temperate parts of the Old World around 800,000 years ago, and ultimately developing into all the cultures in the world today.
>
> From this we postulate an African origin for all mankind. The existence of crude stone tools in Africa a million and a half to two million years ago allows us to suppose the existence of culture at that time. Our guess suggests that the possessor of this culture could not have survived without it; therefore, he

deserves the designation man, however primitive or crude he might have been.[1]

The present discussion concerns itself especially with the Mediterranean World as well as South Africa, East Africa, Central Africa, West Africa, and America. Let me say at the outset that I shall make very little distinction between world religions and the Christian religion as it relates to the concept of God-consciousness. However, points of tensions between the concepts of black people will be in focus, both as religion and culture or slavery and imperialism in Africa, Asia, and in the Americas. *of the black church*

The God-consciousness in this paper is to be understood in terms of universalism. It is in this context that the black church has attempted to free itself from the negative impact of imperial and colonial domination, and has continued through its God-consciousness to witness, not only to the aliveness of Jesus Christ but to the aliveness of God in man, when Jesus Christ is no longer a white man but a universal spirit of truth in all walks of life demanding justice, mercy, understanding of holy love.

The black people of many nations have sought for roots and identity. But where the meetinghouse was less than the church, frustration ensued. And where the true witness of the gospel is replaced by culture, Eastern or Western, it has forced and is compelling the black church historian and theologian to reexamine the cultures and religions of Egypt, the rest of Africa, and Asia, seeking to uncover sources of truth omitted and denied by those who wish to suppress anything constructive that might have evolved from an ethnic setting that was or is predominantly black. The hottest question before the black theologian today is: Was Jesus of Nazareth or of Samaria? black or light?

> "He who comes from God listens to God's words. You, however, are not from God, and this is why you will not listen." The Jews came back at Jesus: "Were we not right in saying that you are a Samaritan and have a demon in you?" "I have no demon," Jesus answered (John 8:47–49).[2]

[1] C. Loring Brace, "The Origin of Man," *Natural History*, The Journal of the American Museum of Natural History, New York City, LXXIX, 1, January 1970, pp. 46 ff.

[2] *Good News for Modern Man* (New York: American Bible Society, 1966).

But notice Jesus did not say that he was not a Samaritan.

One of the major contributions of Egypt to world culture is said to be in the field of religion and life. Egypt was concerned with reconciling conflicting religious systems.[3] In contrast to the culture of the Hebrews, Egyptian culture also generated a sense of security, which bred for the ordinary Egyptian an optimism about life in this world and in the next. He was not a slave to authority; the rules were more inclusive and well understood, with a marked degree of freedom of personality. There was always before him the threat of disaster and the hope for success. "The legend of the seven years of plenty and the seven lean years was no fantasy for Egypt, it was always a threatening possibility." [4]

Contrary to the image that has been created from Hebrew literature and from the suppression and omission of mixed concepts in black Egypt and Africa, it is quite noticeable that near the close of the fourth dynasty a change of the royal family took place. Western papyrus preserved a story which tells how Khufu, a king of the fourth dynasty, was told by a (magician) prophet that a priestess of Ra, the sun god had conceived three sons by the god himself, that they should live to be kings of the land, and that the eldest of them should be high priest of Heliopolis. This came true, and the kings of the fifth dynasty represented a new royal family whose home was Heliopolis and whose religion was therefore that of the life-giving sun. This became the state religion. The pharaohs of this dynasty proclaimed themselves sons of Ra (or Suns of God) and built great new temples in the god's honor and were buried in tombs sacred to the sun at Heliopolis.[5]

It was during this time, about 4241 B.C., that Osiris, the god of the Nile Valley and of resurrection, entered the literature. This concept represented both the spiritual and physical resurrection. This was faith in life, sustained by the giver of life.

Osiris was once in the distant past the king who had "kept the hearts alive" and who now had the responsibility of leading

[3] "The Cambridge Ancient History," Vol. I, T1580 B.C., *Egypt to Babylon* (New York: Macmillan, 1928), pp. 326–27.

[4] John A. Wilson, *The Culture of Ancient Egypt* (Chicago: University of Chicago Press, 1957), pp. 11–12.

[5] "The Cambridge Ancient History," *op. cit.*, pp. 331–33.

his subjects through the crisis of death into an orderly Beyond. Since the old king had been resurrected from the dead, he became king of the dead.[6]

> They are all thine, all those who come to thee,
> Great and Small, they belong to thee,
> Those who live upon earth, they all reach thee,
> Thou art their master, there is none outside thee.[7]

Identification with Osiris led to a desire to imitate his life and good works, and so by his powers to be resurrected from the dead. It also led to ethical and moral principles found in the book commonly known as the Egyptian Book of the Dead,[8] a book that reveals much more about life than about death. Out of the old kingdom were born new ethical standards. Many of them deal with the high moral aspirations of the Egyptians, some of which had already been attained. "My soul shall not be fettered to my body at the gates of the underworld (hell); but I shall enter in peace and shall come forth in peace." [9] Each candidate for the new life after death had to account for his past actions. Could he honestly answer:

> . . . I have not done iniquity.
> . . . I have not robbed with violence.
> . . . I have not done violence to any man.
> . . . I have not committed theft.
> . . . I have not made light the bushel.
> . . . I have not acted deceitfully.
> . . . I have not uttered falsehood.
> . . . I have not defiled the wife of a man.
> . . . I have not encroached upon sacred
>       times and seasons . . .[10]

These expressions and many others are expressions of the God-consciousness in the nature and experience of all men. They are also found in the Tell el-Amarna—or the "Horizons of Aton." God is no longer confined to the Nile Valley but is for all men in all the world. This God-consciousness may be summarized in the poem which I quote from Lewis Browne.

---

[6] Henri Frankfort, *Kingship and the Gods* (Chicago: University of Chicago Press, 1958), p. 207. Copyright 1948 by The University of Chicago.

[7] Ibid., p. 208.

[8] E. A. Wallis Budge, *The Egyptian Book of the Dead* (New York: Dover, 1967), p. ix.

[9] Lewis Browne, *The World's Great Scriptures* (New York: Macmillan, 1946), p. 51. Copyright, 1946, by Lewis Browne.

[10] Ibid., pp. 51–52.

> Thy rising is beautiful, O living Aton,
>     lord of eternity
> Thou art shining, beautiful, strong;
> Thy love is great and mighty,
> Thy rays are cast into every face.
> Thy glowing hue brings life to hearts,
> When thou hast filled the Two Lands with
>     love.
> O God who himself fashioned himself,
> Maker of every land,
> Creator of that which is upon it:
> Men, all cattle large and small,
> All trees that grow in the soil,
> They live when thou dawnest for them
> Thou art the mother and the father of
>     all that Thou hast made.[11]

These religious concepts were expressed not only along the Nile Valley but in most of West, Central, and South Africa. The African along the Guinea Coast of West Africa expressed in his own speech and tongue his system of religion, which consisted of the universal, transcendent God, with lesser gods as his servants. Before the bishops and popes of the fourth century of the Christian era claimed universal control of man, body, mind, and soul, and through the Petrine doctrine subjugated man to a one-way ticket to heaven, purgatory, or hell, the black people on the West Coast of Africa had their own system of heaven under the auspices of their ebony black priest and wise men.

One need only turn to the proverbs and theology of the people themselves to illustrate the point. And in the same connection we have an illustration of their God-consciousness prior to the coming of Christ, and, in many communities, after his coming.

The totem concept of animal nature was ceasing to satisfy the inner yearning of man. Therefore, he was turning to a deeper search for identity. It was this search that led him to the God-consciousness and to the development of signs and symbols in forms of worship—signs and symbols which should have aided in implementing and perpetuating the God-conscious experiences. The mystical and the spiritual led to accommodative symbolism:

[11] Ibid., p. 43.

1. anthropomorphism—God's like I am—a man
2. race, class, culture—"God's chosen people"
3. taboo, heresy, paganism, treason—to preserve the new forms—symbols
4. symbolism—a means to an end, not an end
5. the nature of man—ultimately comprehended through judgment and justice

The God-consciousness as expressed in Ashanti proverbs will not cover the whole spectrum of West African religion but for our purposes they will suffice.

The Ashanti believed that at one time the ONYANKOPON, the Supreme Being, lived near the village and the people, but because of the way he was treated, moved away into the sky. And therefore common people could no longer approach him. The Supreme Being became transcendent. He was represented by his priests, all of whom were subject to him. According to R. Sutherland Rattray:

"[He is] the power, Spirit. . . ."

He is too remote and too powerful to directly have dealings with mankind, but he distributes for their benefit a little of his power, and this spirit of *mana* or power is what is called down by servants specially trained to know its needs and tastes, and having found a faithful priest, and a temporary dwelling on earth, consents at times to live there, and be the intermediary between man and the Supreme Being, from whom it comes [the power spirit] and of whom it is a part.[12]

The Ashanti says:

"If you wish to tell anything to the
Supreme Being, tell it to the winds."

"Each human being's destiny is preordained and the spirit sets out to enter its mother's womb already knowing its destiny."[13] However, each person is free and has access to the Supreme Being. But the paradox is that such a God (ONYANKOPON) is not worshiped in the same way as the Fante worship the lesser gods. The Fante believe that the Supreme Being does not depend upon the praises and favors of men. Therefore, the Fante worshiped gods and ancestors who have temperaments like men. The reason for worshiping them is to gain their favor

---

[12] R. Sutherland Rattray, *Ashanti Proverbs* (Oxford: Clarendon Press, 1916), p. 22. Used by permission of the publisher.
[13] Ibid., pp. 24–25.

and to appease the gods and their ancestors. The Fante view
of God does not allow them to think in terms of original sin as
many Christians have been taught. They do not believe that
man's life begins in sin and must be saved. To the Fante this
concept is contrary to the meaning and purpose of life itself.
Rather the Fante believe that every individual is made pure by
God (who made everything good) and that he has endowed man
with NKRABEA, a destiny, which conditions a person's existence,
and in which each man plays a part in directing his own life.
In other words, NKRABEA is a man's native intelligence which
helps the person to lead a righteous or objective life. In short,
the Fante believe that man has no need for the historical Christ
to save him from original sin which, to him, never happened.[14]

It seems to me that here again we have an expression of
God-consciousness in one of the oldest African cultures on
record.

Though the God-consciousness of the pre-Christian religions
persists and continues to exist even in Christian world culture,
it is not in opposition to the being of Christ or the teachings of
Jesus of Nazareth. John Calvin wrote:

> There is within the human mind, and indeed by natural
> instinct, an awareness of divinity [Divintas Sensum—"Seed of
> Religion"]. . . .
> Since, therefore, men one and all perceive that there is a
> God and that he is their Maker, they are condemned by their
> own testimony because they have failed to honor him and to
> consecrate their lives to his will. . . . Yet there is . . . no na-
> tion so barbarous, no people so savage, that they have not a
> deep-seated conviction that there is a God.[15]

The important point to remember in the Fante religion and
history is that they felt they were strong enough to atone for
their own misdeeds against spirits and their fellowman and
they did not in the least see the need for anyone to have to
suffer in their stead. And in Fante culture has no place for the
deification of human beings. For each human soul is thought

[14] Kodwe E. Ankrah, "Saint Augustine: On the Christianization of the
Uninstructed. A Twentieth-century African's Point of View" (Hartford,
Conn.: Hartford Seminary Foundation, 1961), unpublished research, pp.
24–26.

[15] From *Calvin: Institutes of the Christian Religion* (Vol. I, Bk. 1, pp.
43–44), Vol. XX, The Library of Christian Classics, edited by John T.
McNeill and translated by Ford Lewis Battles. Published in the U.S.A.
by The Westminster Press. Copyright © MCMLX, by W. L. Jenkins. Used
by permission.

to be part of the Supreme God. Besides, each human being works his way closer and closer to God, predicated upon his merits and virtues. Here is the fact of personal salvation. This is salvation finally determined by a man working with God, since man's direct contact is with him all the time.[16]

In fact, in Egypt and West Africa, as well as in the rest of the world, the God-consciousness was and is a stabilizing creative force in the life of man; the black man as well as the white man—European, African, or the black American.

In the words of Olive Schreiner, "Truth is not more truth because it is three thousand years old, nor is it less truth because it is of yesterday. All books which throw light on truth are God's books." [17] If we can accept this assumption, we then have a summary of most of what we have been saying.

The Christian church had its birth in the midst of the great mystery religions. The only man to assist Jesus Christ in carrying the cross was black Simon, a man who was forced to carry the cross. But the most meaningful portion of the drama is that of the resurrection, on the third day. The Christian church has never taken the time or the interest to relate the concept of resurrection in Egyptian experience and faith with the stories told by the frightened and deserting disciples. Is there a relationship between the spiritual resurrection of Paul and that of the God-conscious Egyptians, or the prophet Hosea when he wrote: "Come, and let us return unto the Lord: for he hath torn, and he will heal us; he hath smitten, and he will bind us up. After two days will he revive us: in the third day he will raise us up, and we shall live in his sight (Hosea 6:1–2, KJV)." Could it be true that "the essential truth of the resurrection is the central Egyptian conception of the one life force, the one soul of being, the self-generating, self-sustaining power, ever renewing itself in phenomena"? [18] And is it also true that "the greatest error of conventional religionism is the prevalent idea of a static eternity for man's spirit after departure from earth"? [19]

---

[16] Ankrah, *op. cit.*, p. 27.
[17] Olive Schreiner, *Trooper Peter Halket of Mashonaland* (Boston: Robert Bros., 1897), p. 55.
[18] Alvin B. Kuhn, *The Lost Light* (Elizabeth, N.J.: Academy Press, 1940), pp. 555–56.
[19] Ibid.

The Christian church was born in controversy and persecution. The tension was between Jews who denied Jesus Christ as the Messiah of the Hebrews and the followers of the newly experienced Christ who insisted that he was the fulfillment of the Old Testament prophecy. But above all, there was the culture struggle. In the Greco-Roman or Hellenistic culture there were the tool, the badge, and the Empire; Greek in the East and Latin in the West, together with all the implications of language and symbolism. These made up the culture complex which identified the Greeks and distinguished them from the barbarians. (A dirty word to use against anyone—barbarian.)

The Jews and first-century Christians made up an island of exception to the rules. Christians were regarded as a branch of Judaism or the new religion and began to speak of themselves as a "new race" or "new nation" using these terms interchangeably to mean the same thing.[20]

The Western world ignored the writings of Paul. It not only became fascinated with the political and economic possibilities of the concept of new race or new Israel–new nation but became victimized by it as well. The racial overtones were beyond the ethical morality of church and state. Nor is the sense of guilt allowed to stand in the way when the promotion of race, class, and empire is in question.

In A.D. 403 Epiphanius of Salamia addressed to the church a hymn which was a treatise against heresies:

> Your place is at the King's right hand,
> Your robe is of gold, thin red and em-
> broidered,
> There is no darkness in you. Once you
> were black, but now you have beauty
> and whiteness of skin.
> With you there is safety from heresy's
> hateful designs and shelter from the
> storm it raises with you, holy mother
> church, we take heart again with you
> and with your holy teaching,
> which alone tells us what we may truly
> believe about God.[21]

[20] Buell G. Gallagher, *Color and Conscience: The Irrepressible Conflict* (New York: Harper & Bros., 1946), pp. 41–42.
[21] A. Hamman, ed., *Early Christian Prayers* (Chicago: Regnery Co., 1961), p. 55.

Obviously Africa, Egypt, and the Near East did not find the welcome or the hope in the Roman Empire as did the Germanic and Celtic peoples from Central and Northern Europe; not only were the black people rebuffed by the Empire, they were also forced to reject the church.

The Nestorian Church was cut off from Rome. A church which had at one time ordained bishops for India, her witness stretched from the Mediterranean to the Pacific—even into China. The Nestorian Church had more than 200 bishops, each with separate sees. In cutting itself off from the Nestorian Church, the Church of the Empire had lost contact with the greatest missionary outreach before the nineteenth century.[22]

While in North Africa, west of Egypt and north of the Sahara, Tertullian spoke of the church of the martyrs, defying the Roman Empire.

> We grew up in great numbers, as often as we were cut down by you. The blood of the martyrs is the seed of the Church. We are of yesterday, and yet we have filled every place belonging to your cities, islands, castles, towns, assemblies, your very camps and companies, palace, senate, forum, we leave you your temples only.[23]

With leaders such as the apologist Tertullian, an organizer Cyprian, and a theologian Augustus, the African church once covered what is now Tripoli, Tunisia, Morocco, and Libya. And it is reported to have had 579 bishops presiding over the same number of dioceses.[24] There was even one bishop presiding over the "black huts." But in the seventh century the African and Egyptian churches fell under the sword of Islam. The strength of Islam was in faith and fear. Perhaps more important was the appearance of Islam in its earlier years as a kind of Christian heresy rather than a non-Christian religion. But the basic stability of Islam was that it had little if any race complex. And according to Gallagher: "The total elimination of the African Church from Christendom can be charged squarely to the false identification of Christianity with the purpose of empire." [25] Africa was to Rome only a colonial state in spite of its wealth. Africans were never accepted in the church as equals, always as

[22] Gallagher, *op. cit.*, pp. 44–45.
[23] Apology XXXVII.
[24] Gallagher, *op. cit.*, p. 46.
[25] Ibid., p. 51.

subjects. The rival religion Islam offered equality and inclusiveness instead of exclusiveness. And "with the loss of the Copts and the Berbers, Christianity became, for the first time, a white man's religion." [26] And since this time Christianity has been given a false identification with the white race. The darker people—according to the American classification of Negroes—were given up and lost over to Islam. It is no wonder United States Senator Bilbo, speaking to the Mississippi Legislature, said, "The white man is the Custodian of the Gospel of Jesus Christ."

The fact is that the time from the seventh century until the emancipation proclamation of Abraham Lincoln near the middle of the nineteenth century, a period of more than a thousand years, might easily be called the White Ages of the Dark Church. If the world could be saved only through Jesus Christ, then it was lost; for the so-called custodians of the gospel had taken pride in alienating the black church and peoples from the gospel. Thereafter it is clear to me that the God-consciousness of the black church, which transcends any racial religion or ethnic stock, cannot afford to go on being a replica of an imperical state church, rooted in pride and prejudice. The black church must be redemptive in nature to all mankind. Therefore the black church is called upon to rise to the occasion of witness and prophecy.

It is common knowledge that when the Christians went to war in Spain against the Moors, they combined their defense of empire and religion to establish a tradition and a tool which became a trademark in their conquest and wholesale brutality and robbery in Central and South America. In that struggle religious and racial attitudes were welded into a unique single pattern. And where nonwhites were converted they were to share a subordinate role in the new religion of Christians, since they were enjoying a lower status in the eyes of God and man.[27]

There was not a nonwhite church in Christendom to cry out against the false identification of Christianity and the new imperialism.[28] This part of world history and church history is

26 Ibid., p. 52.
27 Ibid., p. 54.
28 Ibid., pp. 54–55.

under review and scrutiny by the black church in its search for a new ground of being on which to reestablish a God-consciousness predicated on the fatherhood of God and the sinner, man, based upon the experiences of Blacks, and the teachings of Jesus and life.

The Old Testament must be ruled out on the basis of the fact that the Old Testament gave the New England settlers the concept of their being the chosen people, and the Old Testament deity as the God of Warfare. In this manner religious sanction was gained not only for seizing the land from the people, the Indians, but to make room for the new Israel. Thus, the Old Testament must be reevaluated in the light of world religions and modern scholarship.

The Reformation seems to have made little if any difference as to how the Puritans of Massachusetts or the Anglicans of Virginia or the Catholics of Maryland treated the American Indian or the black man from Africa. But there was a difference in the attitude and action of the dissenting Quakers and Baptists in Rhode Island and Pennsylvania, toward the Indians and Blacks or Negroes on the American continent. The same can be said as it relates to Africa.[29]

The fact is that Christianity on the whole has been identified with the aspirations of white men in every part of the world —especially the merchants and explorers. This is true in the Americas, in Africa, as well as in the Near East and Far East, and wherever and whenever Christianity has prostituted itself to any form of imperialism, gaining empires and loosing the humanity of all shades and colors, especially black and white.

Prior to the Protestant Reformation the only ray of hope was found in mysticism, pietism, and spiritualism, in Wycliffe, Huss, and other such men with a Christian commitment and dedication. Following the Reformation, this hope was expanded by the radical reformers in Europe, the Methodist movement in England, and the early American settlement—a movement flanked by the Baptists and Quakers.[30]

There was still another ray of hope in the birth of the mis-

[29] Ibid., p. 55.
[30] George H. Williams, *The Radical Reformation* (Philadelphia: Westminster Press, 1962), p. xix.

sionary enterprise. But it was seized upon and placed under a bushel basket when the Portuguese in 1482 discovered the Congo River, followed by a missionary expedition to establish the Catholic Church in 1490. Thus, state and church joined hands to suppress individual growth and development. Once the missionary possibilities were established, the Jesuits built their missionary stations. The Protestants baptized a number of slaves and sought to establish a number of missions, and by 1685 the Huguenots entered the colony.

In 1737, English Moravian missions were established in South Africa.[31] The economic value of the slave trade and enmity between the European powers caused the world to witness the most diabolical expression of man's inhumanity to man. It was during the eighteenth and nineteenth centuries that the image of the African and American Blacks or Negroes were reduced from that of "a man," a child of God, to an animal and a "thing," to be bought and sold on any market, for any given price, to the highest bidder.

It is important to observe that in 1876, only 10 percent of Africa was occupied by Europeans; by 1885, 25 percent was occupied. The event which made possible the "rape of Africa" was the Berlin Conference of 1818–85, which legalized for the Europeans the partitioning of Africa among the European powers, with special concessions being made to Leopold of Belgium in the Congo. In less than fifteen years, from 1876 to 1890, the European powers increased their control of African territory fivefold, leaving one fifth of the territory—still fivefold—to be divided by the end of the nineteenth century. Of the total superficial area of Africa, only one fifth remained to be divided when the century closed.

The tragedy of these actions led us into two world wars. And the blessing has been a confidence in a single moral universe and especially in a black awareness of the distorted imperial state church. It has also led the American black church as well as the black church in Africa and Asia to conclude that no Christianity can be genuine when it substitutes European

---

[31] G. C. Oosthuizen, *Post Christianity in Africa* (Grand Rapids: Eerdmans, 1967), p. 2. Used by permission.

culture for the teachings of Jesus and the love of God. The church's failure to act with love and to be a fellowship has tended to alienate it from those whom the church proposes to save. According to Oosthuizen:

> Outstanding men in Africa have deeply pondered this problem, men such as Westermann, Willoughby, Tucker, Shropshire, Gutamann, and Edwin Smith. They tried to stem the tide of the church's prevalent attitude to the cultural heritage of the inhabitants of Africa. . . . The tribal culture of the Chagga, as indeed that of any other people, is actually the manifestation of an inner spirit . . . ordained by God.[32]

Both in Africa and America, the Negro and the African have been disturbed by the tension created in the imperial church's witness on the one hand versus fellowship and love on the other. The church has also separated itself from the national aspirations of the nationals of Africa and the democratic aspirations of Afro-Americans. According to David B. Barrett:

> This failure of the version of Christianity proclaimed by the missions has been three fold. . . . In the first place, the failure to practice love as understanding led to a disastrous absence of the scriptural quality of Philadelphia or Brotherly love. . . . Secondly, lack of brotherly contact with Africans led directly to a failure to understand Africanism (the whole traditional complex) sufficiently well to differentiate the good elements from the bad. . . . The third failure was even more serious for missions who professed complete allegiance to the scriptures. Failing to understand Africanism, they failed to discern the existence of any link between traditional society and Biblical faith . . .[33]

On the American scene, those churches that have been loudest in emphasizing the Bible have also been the most reactionary in recognizing civil rights and practicing democracy. They have been the first to condemn such movements for reform and have led in persecuting any of their pastors who might be identified with such an activity as voter registration or sit-ins. In other words there is no relationship between the fellowship or witness of the denomination or congregation and the aspirations of people toward a better standard of living. And the norm for all worship has been predicated upon the norms of the imperial state church, free of any conviction of Christian ethic.

---

[32] Ibid., pp. 3 f.

[33] David B. Barrett, *Schism & Renewal in Africa: An Analysis of Six Thousand Contemporary Religious Movements* (Nairobi: Oxford University Press, 1968), pp. 156–57.

Many black churches have fallen into this trap. In such situations there remains little if any incentive for creativity or sense
of personal belonging or place for expression and encounter
where these might be needed most. It was this type of situation
that led to the organization of the black church in America, in
which there seems to have been in the eighteenth century a
deep sense of God-consciousness, expressed in protest against
injustices and other forms of social and moral evil in the establishment.

This was the period when integration of churches gave way
to segregation of churches, when ecumenical patterns were
abolished for denominationalism on the part of black and white
churches in America. It was both a God-consciousness as well as
race and class consciousness that produced our separatist
churches both in America and in Africa. And in Africa even the
American black bishops did not understand the nature and function of African culture. Such a lack of understanding caused
Bishop J. B. Small of the African Methodist Episcopal Zion
Church to refuse the admission of the Ethiopian Church because the Ethiopian Church practiced polygamy as part of the
economy. The Ethiopian Church today is one of the strongest
in South Africa.

The overthrow of Bishop Crowther in Nigeria led to the
establishment of separatist African churches, both Methodist
and Anglican. This was not due to religious efforts, but an attempt was made by the authorities to prevent the continuous
growth and establishment of a middle class. Crowther empha-
sized the material values of having village schools. The authorities wanted only the children of chiefs to attend mission schools.
Many missionaries and government officials thought that the
mission schools were not good for the common children. However, the village school became important for developing a middle class in Africa.[34] On the American scene in rural areas, the
Negro or black church furnished the only neighborhood school
for primary education. On the other hand the denominational
normal and junior college prepared preachers, teachers, doctors,

---

[34] J. F. A. Ajayi, *Christian Missions in Nigeria: 1841–1891* (Evanston:
Northwestern University Press, 1965), pp. 229–72.

lawyers, dentists, who formed the American middle class. The educational program of the establishment was geared to serve mulattoes on the whole and special servant classes during the first seventy-five to one hundred years. There were many dedicated teachers who were white in many of these schools. This was another ray of hope in spite of paternalistic spirits that prevailed.

But in America, the black church was aware of its need for community and national leadership. Therefore schools were organized such as Atlanta University, Wilberforce University, Livingstone College, Arkansas Baptist, Lane College, only to name a few, with theological and liberal arts training classes. This type of institution for many years helped those men and women who by all other standards were beyond help. The "late bloomer" became one of the most beautiful of all the trees of the forest. Yes, African and American theological education has been like the "late bloomers," but today we see a new forest of giant oaks growing. We also see a forest of ebonies growing to full size in Africa and America.

In America, we are now aware of the wisdom of Bishop James W. Hood, who said in substance, "When the white church removes the causes which drove us out, then we will return." For the black church in America is the result of a class structure. The God-consciousness of the black church in Africa and America must be accepted as a valid norm for equality and dialogue.

In Africa the growing, thriving separatist churches, over 6,000 in number, bear new witness and expression of the God-consciousness in terms of cultural traits as well as ancestral patterns. They have an awareness that African and Negro ancestors were men of faith as vital to their race as the Hebrew ancestors were to theirs. Those who fought and died in South Africa, those who died fighting the British over the Golden Stool, as well as those who died in the Civil War are martyrs for the faith in the Supreme God—the one and only God. All died in their faith in the one and only God. Hebrews told us not to have any other God before him; the African insists that there is no other supreme being to have. There is only one.

And in Yorubaland between 1890 and 1920, the African

church posed as the conscience of the mission churches, re-
minding them again and again of the progressive philosophy
that the missions themselves once held and which they still
professed to hold. It should be noted that these policies varied
from national territory to national community. But the British
tended to be less harsh, more sedate, giving more freedom
within the colonial imperial system. The African church as an
effective alternative to the mission, became a guarantor of tol-
erance within mission Christianity. It was the presence of the
African church that put an end to mass excommunications. The
African church was a powerful check against the moralist-purist
who attempted to deny the African a top place because of "morals." They broke the back of the gentleman's agreements of
comity and forced a more widespread distribution of educational facilities than the missions had been willing to undertake.
They also introduced music into services of worship, a practice
later copied by some missions. They also kept alive a literary
ferment and forced Africans to consider carefully the negative
effects of the penetration of Christianity into their culture. And
finally, they stood for a certain type of God-conscious honesty
which was in danger of being overlooked.[35] The African church
has made and is making a tremendous contribution to truth-
seeking through honest God-consciousness.

The black church in America has been one of the vital factors in the birth and growth of the African church. Of particular
importance were the Baptists from Richmond, Virginia and New
York City; Lott Carey in Liberia; the A.M.E. Church in South
Africa; Bishop H. M. Turner; and others. The A.M.E. Zion in
Liberia and the Gold Coast, Bishop John Bryant Small, and
others not only paved the way for an expression of protest
against the imperial powers and state church but also created
an atmosphere where national pastors and leaders could develop in black educational institutions in America.[36]

If we are to move toward a new church, this church must
be predicated upon a genuine God-consciousness through truth

[35] James Bertin Webster, *The African Churches Among the Youba:
1888–1922* (Oxford: Clarendon Press, 1964), pp. 195–98.
[36] B. G. M. Sundkler, *The Bantu Prophets in South Africa* (New York:
Oxford University Press, 1964), pp. 40–42.

and encounter, encounter with people, people who need a new approach to the age-old question of man's relationship to God and God's relationship to man, and man's responsibility to man. A new approach was demonstrated by the black church when, in 1966, the National Committee of Negro Churchmen met at the Statue of Liberty and issued a statement giving its views on the "critical issues" facing the nation at election time. The document concluded, in part:

> We submit that the resolution of the crisis which is upon us requires a change in the nation's priorities. The welfare and dignity of all Americans is more important than the priorities being given to military expansion, space exploration or the production of supersonic jet airliners. . . .
>
> We further call upon white churchmen to join us by endeavoring to mobilize the resources of the white community in completing with us the task at hand. . . .
>
> Again we say: America is at the crossroad. Either we become the democracy we can become, or we tread the path to self-destruction.[37]

[37] Black Power Statement, National Committee of Negro Churchmen, November 3, 1966. At a convocation in St. Louis in 1968, the name of the committee was changed to National Committee of Black Churchmen.

# Chapter Four

# BLACK CONSCIOUSNESS IN THEOLOGICAL PERSPECTIVE

*J. Deotis Roberts, Sr.*

## I. Introduction: Why a Black Theology?

There has arisen most recently a crying need to interpret the spiritual dimensions of the Negro's [1] self-awareness in theological perspective. Within the past few years, the intensity of the "black experience" has deepened and widened. More specifically in the late 60's after the cry for Black Power had echoed throughout the land, the need for a reassessment of all experiences and relationships affecting the destiny of black men in the United States became apparent. It is not surprising that a great deal is being said about a "black theology."

Some attention should first be given to what is meant by a black theology and thus provide some guidelines for the task set before one who seeks to formulate such a statement of the Christian faith. It is to be assumed that a working definition of both "theology" and "blackness" can be found and that these meanings can be combined.

The title of this essay is descriptive of what we have in mind. "Black consciousness" or "black awareness" describe something of the concern which presents itself to us. We are assuming that the black man in the United States has undergone a certain kind of treatment which has produced a unique type of spiritual experience both personal and collective—an experience which deserves theological analysis and interpretation.

---

[1] Throughout this essay "black" and "Negro" will be used interchangeably. Due to the current attractiveness of "black" as a frame of reference for Afro-Americans, this will be most frequently used. All reasons thus far given for using "black" rather than other possible designations have not been convincing. Therefore, it appears to me that "black" is a fad-type usage which was once shunned but is much used for the present.

The Negro's experience is similar to Israel's experience of Egyptian bondage, to give only one example.

We will venture further to say that this experience is not only a matter of psychology but of *live* history. We have the witness of our ancestors, many of whom were slaves, and others, who together with us, have been victims of all types of discrimination (open, legal, subtle, and violent) even after the so-called emancipation. We have a "cloud of witnesses" to substantiate these claims. The souls of black men have been tried and tested in the fires of suffering. We have endured incessant and undeserved infliction of pain due to our blackness. Thus, when we become conscious or aware of our blackness which accounts for this experience inflicted upon us by those who are white and who treat us thus because of the color of our skin, then we must attempt to make sense of our black experience. As Christians we must make theological sense out of our experience if we are to be both black and Christian. Our theological task is to determine what it means to be at once black and Christian in the United States.

Our blackness is a given thing. We are born black and in view of this, no choice is open to us. We have sought to escape our blackness. Some through "passing" by virtue of light skin into white society, some by seeking to belong through achievements in various fields, and some through extreme hedonism or spiritual otherworldliness. I am reminded of a Negro high society woman who moved out of an all-black neighborhood in Chicago into an integrated neighborhood and who sent word back to her brothers and sisters: "Remember, I am thinking about you." Some have sought to escape through interracial marriage—this is especially true of athletes and entertainers who have more money and popularity than learning and insight. *The Great White Hope* is a dramatic presentation of the tragedy that often results. Even if man and wife are able to accept each other, the American society rejects them and their offspring. In a word, the black man in America confronts a *No Exit* sign in reference to his blackness.

The events of the past few years have made us painfully aware that we must face our blackness. The Ph.D's and the no-D's, the haves and the have-nots, are all considered second-class citizens in a white man's world. Whether we live on the Gold Coast or in the dark ghetto, whether we are a "first" in some distinguished post or a garbage collector, to the white man the Negro is still "boss," "boy," or any number of insulting or humiliating titles. We are all united in our blackness and are therefore treated and considered as inherently inferior.

The black man in recent years has become color-conscious in the sense that he is aware that he is black and that to the white majority which controls both the wealth and power in this country, he is not equal. This means that any white man, however poor or illiterate, may assume superiority over any black man whatever his wealth, education, or position. Prejudice is a prejudgment at sight, and the black man is highly visible. Blackness is a fact of life for the Negro. It is a given, it must be accepted—it cannot be ignored, escaped, or overcome. Acceptance of blackness is the only healthy stance for the black man. In Tillichian language, "he must have the courage to be 'black.' " One of the most wholesome and positive aspects of the black revolution is the assertion that "black is beautiful" and that we should seek "black pride." In a city in which well over half of the citizens are black, all the beauty queens are white. In spite of all evidence to the contrary, presented by the white majority, we need to be able to tell our daughters that they are black but they are also beautiful. Only in this way may we find our way to self-identity and self-acceptance.

On the one hand, blackness is ours by birth and, on the other, the Christian faith is ours by choice. What rationale may we give for a black man accepting the Christian faith? A white student recently asked me the key questions: "What," she asked, "is a black theology?" "How does a black theology differ from any other theology?" If the term theology is used in a respectable academic sense and not in a popular or journalistic sense, these questions present a serious challenge to professional theologians.

II. The Nature and Scope of a Black Theology

John MacQuarrie describes theology as God-talk. Theology is theocentric. It must deal with the question of God. It also has some real concern regarding God's dealings with man. Theology includes anthropology which treats the nature and destiny of man. Paul Tillich reminds us that theology is a combination of two Greek words: "theos" (God) and "logos" (reason). Theology is reasoning about God. Theology is a study about God and about man's nature and destiny. It includes man's relation to God and to his fellowman. Christian theology treats these concerns in the context of Christian affirmations. Both philosophy and theology are concerned with ultimate questions. Whereas the philosopher may relate his presuppositions broadly to all religious experiences, a theologian must apply his faith-claims narrowly in his own theological circle, as a Christian, Muslim, or Hindu. It is our task to present a Christian theological perspective.

There is one further preliminary consideration. What method may we use with the best results? There is a real question as to whether any dogmatic or systematic method is adequate for this purpose. All major theologians have been white and, therefore, their dogmas and systems have not been informed by the black experience. The metaphysical approaches to theology have a tendency to be conceptual and inadequately experiential for this task. It is not possible for a nonblack theologian to completely empathize with the black man however compassionate his concern. What we need is a method highly sensitive to experience, but well-informed by abstract thought as well as Christian history and life. Social psychology and ethics will be extremely important instruments. It will be a revolutionary or political theology similar to the theology of hope. It will be a situational or existential theology and it will be a theological ethics due to the serious moral questions raised by racism. A black theology must have deep roots in Christian history and biblical faith if it is to be more than another theological fad. It must be apologetic in the best meaning of this august tradition in theology. There must be an openness to truth whether personal, social, or spiritual in character. A black theology must be an "answering theology" in the Tillichian sense. The questions raised by the "situation of racism" in the United States calls forth a need for a Christian answer, theologically speaking, to the black man's bitter experiences in this country.

The justification for such an endeavor as the development of a black theology is that the black man must find some theological meaning in the Christian faith if he is to be faithful and honest to his commitment or find it in another faith-claim. Some black men are now turning to classical Islam. Scores of black men find it difficult to maintain their faith in the Christian faith simply because they inherited it from their white slave masters. This is true of the "black denominations" as of all others. They separated from their respective parent bodies for racial or sociological reasons rather than on theological grounds. There have been no breakthroughs by black scholars in theology. We have produced no Barths, Tillichs, or Bultmanns. As Christians we have remained down to the present stepchildren to the WASPS in the theological field. We have no theologians and no creeds of our own. We have no formulations or affirmations of faith that reflect our peculiar experience in American life. This explains the almost pathological longing at the present time for a black theology. But where are the theologians? Blackness alone, the call to the ministry will not equip us to be theologians. We need a crash program in the preparation of theologians. We need dedicated hearts and the best minds to pursue this task.

If Karl Barth could look at Nazi Germany and the European crisis in the first quarter of this century and write his triumphant *Commentary on Romans;* if Jürgen Moltmann, several years later can look at postwar Europe and the East-West split and develop his theology of hope; if young radical American theologians can observe the loss of faith in a transcendent God in a society "come of age" in economic success and technological skills, and write the death-of-God theologies, then why cannot a black theologian do his own thing? Even though white American theologians are informed by European insights, they seek to give theological interpretation to suburbia, science, technology, and affluence. These theologies, whether "radical," "secular," or "socio-technic"—though existential, situational, and apologetic—are not aimed at the "dark ghetto" and usually make no real contact with the total experience of any black man, however educated or affluent. They are theologies for "haves"; they have little to offer the "have-nots" for they are based on the white experience of wealth, privilege, and first-class citizenship. Because of racism in American life, there is a *real* black experience of which only the black Christian is truly and fully aware. This, too, needs theological interpretation. I was the only Negro in a small group of Americans abroad several years ago who were honestly seeking to be understanding in race relations. Once I was asked: "Why is it that Negroes seem to think that there is only one problem—race? There are many other problems." My answer was and still is that the black man in this country faces one problem—Race. All other concerns center in this one experience.

We have now made our case for putting black consciousness in theological perspective. To sum up our reasoning we have made several points. We have pointed to the undeserved suffering of the black man in America. We have described the black experience and set it over against our theological task. Our justification for a black theology is based upon the primary need of all enlightened Christians to think theologically about their affirmation of faith. The need "to love God with all our minds" as well as to *feel* God within our hearts, creates a demand for hard and sound theological thinking for all Christians. The black revolution with its emphasis on self-awareness—the affirmation of our blackness as a given fact of daily life—makes this demand most urgent. We must discover the meaning which Christian theology can provide for our black experience in America. Our search is timely and crucial. We must weigh the claims of Christian doctrine in the framework of our black experience. Will we find it to be the answering-theology we need for the deep questions of our existence as black people?

In a time of black-white confrontation and in a period when black men are willing to stand up to life, an escapist and sentimental Jesusology is not the answer. If the Christian faith has an answer, we must not only discover it and interpret it, but we must likewise find a way to communicate it to our brothers trapped in the dark ghetto, to the black bourgeoisie on the Gold Coast and, indeed, to the poverty-stricken and disinherited millions around the globe. All black men, in particular, share the same experience and all need a gospel of deliverance and hope. The time of need is now. Much attention has been given to the test which the Christian faith confronts in the suburbs among the "haves." The real trial of our faith is in pockets of poverty, in the dark ghettos, and among all black people in this country. We now turn to our theological task.

III. The Constructive Phase of a Black Theology

There are certain crucial problems with which the Negro Christian must deal if his faith is to be firmly established and if he is to give adequate justification for the intellectual content of his faith. The problem of God presents itself to the Negro in a unique manner. The existence, absence, and silence of God do not raise the same issues for black Christians as they do for affluent white Christians—or for "poor Whites"; for after all they are white and whiteness has priority in American life. The providence of God, the moral attributes of God, evil and God, the nearness and distance of God, are some of the important elements for forging a doctrine of God which relates to the black experience.

The questions arising from "a man come of age," of "living as if God were not," secularity and God—indeed, the so-called radical theology movement which addresses itself primarily to those who have too much, makes little contact with those who have too little. Thus far no black man has flown in orbit around the moon. Theological problems arising from such breakthroughs are of little interest to black men. The problems of existence keep his attention securely anchored to the earth. Black theology cannot indulge in the problems of interplanetary travel or the communication between humans and whatever beings there may be in outer space; whatever beings or God there may be in outer space must be white anyway. The problems arising from abundant human achievement, self-adequacy, and self-sufficiency do not plague the black man. Even the black man who has arrived intellectually and professionally into middle-class status should be aware that there is an element of grace in his ascendency. Radical theology, whether death-of-God, secularist, sociotechnic, or process, has little appeal to black men with their backs against the wall. Most black intellectuals are more likely to be militant atheists (antitheists) or fundamentalists than Christian humanists or Christian atheists.

The black Christian generally assumes that God exists. He

often asks the poignant questions: Does God care? Is God just, loving, merciful? Is God all-powerful? Why does he permit undeserved suffering? Is God near? Does he watch over all men?

The question of providence is a serious one for black theology. If faith is to be both comforting and meaningful to the black man in the United States, he must be assured that the God of the Christian creed is a benevolent and provident God. The black man must place his trust in a gracious God who superintends all his creatures. The absence of God is of academic interest, but the *presence* of God is an abiding existential concern. This is perhaps why black Christians have received so much inspiration and comfort from the Old Testament which tells how God dwells among his people and cares for them. The God of Abraham, Isaac, and Jacob is a living and present God. In the words of the psalmist, God is a "present help in trouble (Ps. 46:1)." It is rather easy to understand why black slaves and their descendants have found comfort and assurance in the Old Testament. The witness and activity of the Holy Spirit as seen in the New Testament can be of equal inspiration to the black Christian. The Holy Spirit, God dwelling within the New Israel, the church, is Life-giver, Comforter, Guide, and Strengthener. The God of Jesus who identified himself with those of low estate, must be a God who cares for and loves all men. Jesus, "a prince in beggar's garments," is born in a barn and dies on a cross. In birth, death, as in life, he casts his lot with the needy, the sinful, and the disinherited. The God of the Bible is a gracious and provident God. A black theology must develop this theme of a God who is ever-present, a God who cares, who rules, who guides and gives us "strength for the day." But this God must no longer be understood as a means of escape from life, but as one who enables us to stand up to life. The God of comfort and succor is likewise a God of power and challenge. The thrust of the doctrine of providence must not be life-negating, but life-affirming. Black theology, in asserting the presence of God, must be positive and aggressive, rather than passive, quietistic, and escapist.

Providence and creation are inseparably linked. The black man needs to know that the God of Christian faith is "the author of nature" and that, in spite of the evil and ugliness in his experience, creation is beautiful and good. The black Christian needs to have clearly presented the distinction between man's disorder and God's design. Black theology will betray the black man if it undergirds the theme: "You may have all this world and give me Jesus." Creation and all its benefits have been given to man for his enrichment and fulfillment. At this point the black theologian needs to be informed by secularity. Black people, like white people in this country, are obsessed with things as ends in themselves. Things for many black people are the *esse* (essence) of life rather than for the *bene esse* (well-being) of life. Secularism as a God-substitute (the worship of material things—or in some cases the practice of child-worship) as a quasi-religious manifestation, has overtaken all Americans —black and white. The concept of secularity emphasizes this world as a place where God is present. God as Author of nature, as Lord and Judge of creation and history, is in the here and now. Black theology must say *yes* to *this* life and the order of creation which sustains it. This affirmative doctrine of creation is a sheer necessity if black men are to have a healthy approach to the goods and services which make the present life full and abundant.

The affirmative embracement of the present life does not require a rejection of a belief in the future life. There is some real advantage in seeing the present life from the vantage point of eternity. What I am suggesting is a rejection of both "pie in the sky" and "loaves and fishes." I am suggesting a life of quality instead of a life based on quantity both here and hereafter. There is in this connection a great need to unite faith and ethics. A rejection of a valid theology often leads to the abandonment of a valid ethic. Frequently, all we have left is expediency in which one individual seeks to have his own way at the expense of his own peer group. I was not really surprised to see a sign changed in a riot-torn neighborhood from "Black Power" to "black respect" with the comment: "Stop killing your own people!" If those who advocated naked Black Power had a theological understanding of man, they would have been less optimistic and more realistic concerning human nature at the outset.

The moral integrity of the Divine Character has real possibilities for a black theology. Against the consciousness of unjust treatment, an unloving relationship based on racism, and the painful awareness of an unmerciful society, there is a need to believe that God is just, loving, and merciful. This is the reason, I believe, why the Old Testament prophets have had a special place in the hearts of black men. Amos' message of social justice sent from a God of justice, Isaiah's condemnation of the feast days of those whose hands are full of blood, and Micah's list of divine requirements—do justly, love mercy, and walk humbly with God—have spoken to the heart of the Negro. Then, Jesus, who came not to destroy the law and the prophets but to fulfill the promise by his life, his teachings, and his cross, demonstrates the very life of this God. Thus as scriptures are "opened up" and as we are made to see the will of God in the teachings of the prophets and the very life and example of the Son of God in the incarnation, there unfolds before us the possibility of a black theology which assures us that God in his very nature is love, justice, and mercy. The God who is love is lovingly just and his love embraces his mercy. Thus amidst all the abuses, exploitation, and injustice so abundant in our midst, we have the assurance that the benevolent, provident God in whom we trust, is loving, just, and merciful and that all evidence to the contrary, this God who is lord over life and lord of history will have the last word.

A God in process is "becoming" rather than "being." He is in some sense incomplete, though related to man's experience. The Whiteheadian God—"a principle of concreteness"—the God of neoclassical theism (Hartshorne's God) may provide intellectual satisfaction for those preoccupied with the metaphysical problems of the absoluteness and relatedness of God, but black theology must concern itself with more experiential matters. Ours must be a theology of involvement. The biblical paradox of transcendence-imminence sums up for us the nearness and distance of God. It is more important for black theology that God be omnipotent—that is, all-powerful—than it is that we work out an intellectually satisfying metaphysical statement of absoluteness-relatedness in a panentheistic statement in which God is no longer being but becoming. This task is proceeding on schedule in the writings of Cobb, Odgen, Hartshorne, Christian,

Daniel Day Williams, and others. What we need as black men is to know that God embodies the highest ethical virtues and that he has sufficient power to undergird his moral attributes.

Since the theme of "power" figures so largely in black consciousness, it is important to have a close theological look at this concept. Self-determination over against determination and power over against powerlessness are at the heart of all revolutions of our time. Beginning with the Christian understanding of God, what light may we cast upon this aspect of black awareness? The black man, who lives in the dark ghetto, in a rented shack, and who works under a white boss, whose environment is regulated from city hall, whose landlord is white or Jewish and lives in the suburbs, lives an other-directed, powerless life. What does the Christian understanding of God say to this man whose life is controlled by a white landlord, a white boss, and white politicians? A few years back this man was "happy" in his plight, but now that Black Power has been proclaimed, he is aware and he is angry. Even if he can find "passification" through wine, women, and song, on the one hand, and "spiritual aspirins," on the other, this is his *real* condition. What does the Christian faith have to say about God, man, and community which can make a difference to this man and his children?

Power, as such, is morally neutral. The use of power determines its moral content. Both Hitler and Gandhi used power. Hitler accepted Nietzsche's principle, "might makes right." He, therefore, asserted that the "strong do what they will" and "the weak endure what they must." Hitler used for his ends naked and brutal military force and violence. Gandhi challenged the British raj and won independence for the Indian people by another form of power. It was based upon ahimsa, or noninjury. It has as its basis reverence for life. It is rooted in Hindu scripture, but is more pronounced in the Jiana and Buddhist sacred texts. Gandhi called it *satya-graha,* truth or soul-force. Martin Luther King, Jr., inspired by both Gandhi and Jesus, referred to it as agape, love. This power is expressed through non-cooperation and demonstrations in reference to social evils. Power, therefore, is an *instrumental virtue* when used for good ends, but it may degenerate into an *instrumental vice* when used for evil purposes. Love and goodness, on the other hand, are *intrinsic* virtues.

God is all-powerful, but his unlimited power is consistent with his character. It is indispensable to a worthy doctrine of providence to be assured that God has sufficient power to back up his love, justice, and mercy. A finite God or rather a finite-infinite God—a God limited in power, but absolute in goodness (Brightman's God)—is said to be in touch with our infirmities. He is near and related in that he has an impediment or a disability in his own nature over which his will has no control. He moves from an "eternal crucifixion to an eternal Easter," but this God is not adequate for the faith we need to confront the black experience. A God infinite in goodness, but finite in power does not satisfy an oppressed people. Black men need the assurance that God has sufficient power to sustain his love and justice. We need to know that there is no evil in the nature of God: that all evil is external to him. We need the assurance that this God is not capricious or arbitrary in the exercise of will or power, that he is benevolent and morally upright. We need to know that he never misuses or abuses his power and that his power is instrumental to his love and justice. When asked by a Muslim why I accept Jehovah rather than Allah, I could answer forthrightly that it is my understanding of God which gives me confidence in the Christian message.

Evil and God is another problem that must claim the attention of the theologian of the black experience. Any easy theoretical solution to the omnipresent fact of undeserved suffering will not suffice. The cross of Christian experience is no stranger to the life of the black Christian. Such themes as "God almighty and ills unlimited," "evil and the love of God," and "the cross in Christian experience" are not theoretical but experiential to black men. The questions: Why do the righteous suffer and the evil prosper? What is the meaning of physical pain and mental agony? These and related questions haunt the souls of black folk. What theological interpretation of evil will bring comfort and assurance to black people, enabling them to embrace the Christian style of life?

Here we are concerned primarily with moral evil as distinguished from physical pain. Any solution to this problem which attempts to explain evil away or which treats it as an illusion, will not suffice. The implication that all suffering is deserved and serves a useful purpose as a discipline, misses the mark also. I have seen the visible hate on the faces of white men whose faces were reddened by my black but nameless presence. These men had come to hate a black man on sight. To the black man moral evil is real. His own black community is a "human jungle" and he is the constant victim of exploitation and abuse by white men. Moral evil is not an illusion; it is not based upon desert, but it is real and it must be faced.

Human freedom perverted by self-centeredness and selfish inhumanity resulting from sin points us in the right direction. Even so, the existence and persistence of evil in a world created, guided, and sustained by a benevolent, gracious, compassionate, and provident God said to be absolutely good and all-powerful, is difficult to overcome in theological discourse.

A realistic view of man as sinner together with an understanding of the depths of collective sin as well as personal pride and estrangement, provides some insight into this problem. A black theology must somehow maintain trust in the absolute goodness and omnipotence of God notwithstanding the fact of moral evil (both personal and social) against which we must struggle. We must confront evil and find through the resources of our faith the wherewithal to stand up to life. The character of the God in whom we put our trust, must be sufficient for our need.

The drama of Job is an excellent existential analysis of our black experience, but Job's theological solution—"a God whose ways are past finding out"—is no longer very comforting. Many theological statements, like Job's friends and mourners, have brought "false comfort" to the black man in his suffering. Is it possible for the Easter message to speak to the black experience? I believe that it is. The Christian faith is not one of escape, but of confrontation and overcoming. Jesus went *to* Jerusalem, not *around* Jerusalem, in spite of the cross that awaited him there. The cross is at once the symbol of confrontation of evil at its worst with holiness at its best, and the manifestation of "love divine, all loves excelling." The empty tomb is testimony to the *overcoming* power of love which takes us *through* and *beyond* the hold which evil and death have upon us. The grace of the cross and the power of the resurrection are the basis of our believing hope. The faith we need is that the God who is able to bring strength out of weakness will by his sanctifying grace, transform our lives in such wise that the cross in our experience may be a way that leads to victory rather than defeat.

According to our faith, it is the Son of man who suffers vicariously for human redemption. The Son of man title of Jesus refers to a heavenly or original man: man in a perfect sense and therefore man as he ought to be. This is a title of exaltation. The suffering servant title of Jesus refers to his suffering on behalf of others. It is related to Deutero-Isaiah's servant passage which states that "by his stripes we are healed." The suffering servant title refers to humiliation, undeserved suffering that is to be redemptive. Suffering is the means to redemption. Exaltation and humiliation are united in Christology. It is the Son of man who suffers redemptively for the salvation of mankind. As those who know the depths of undeserved suffering, may we somehow find a clue to its meaning in the example of Christ. To seek suffering as an end in itself is to court an empty and meaningless martyrdom. But to transform suffering into a moral and spiritual victory over evil is to live redemptively: it is to use the suffering which is ours rather than to be used by it.

Within the framework of a brief lecture, we cannot tackle a comprehensive black theology. What we have attempted here is representative and may serve as a guide to a fuller formulation. Having looked at some considerations we must give to a doctrine of God, we now turn to a brief consideration of human nature and destiny.

We have mentioned earlier the need to have a realistic view of human nature. Black theology must take sin seriously. Man is born morally neutral. He is neither inherently good nor evil, but potentially either, depending upon maturation and learning. Both heredity and environment play an important part in the direction of life. Man created in the image of God is a rational and free being. His responsibility and guilt are personal. Each

man is the Adam of his own soul. Man's dignity is his birth-
right: it is God-given. A black man, as all other men, is born
dignified, free, and equal. He does not need to earn the right to
be treated as a human being. A complex, whether inferior or
superior, is psychological and sociological, but not Christian
theological.

Even though the Christian understanding of man needs
to be informed by all other interpretations of human life, it is
unique. Man, according to the Christian faith, is born into a
sinful environment and is shaped by it, but because he is self-
determined, he may rise above his environment and even redeem it. The Christian view of man is realistic: "All have
sinned." This is the explanation for the brokenness between
man and man. Sin is moral evil, but moral evil results from a
prior estrangement between a man and his God. According to
the Christian understanding the slums must be cleaned up, but
the heart must be purified also.

Sin is both personal and social. The evangelicals deal
mainly with personal sins, while the liberals are concerned primarily with collective sins. For example, hippies who are known
for loose living, are very much concerned about Vietnam and
civil rights. In a more serious vein, Quakers and Unitarians are
generally considered as liberal in a theological sense, but they
are usually social activists. On the other hand, Baptists, Methodists, and others who insist on "sound doctrine" are often in-
different when it comes to human rights of another race or class.
A Christian realism in reference to the understanding of man
combines the concern for a sound theology with radical concern
and action. Man's sinful life must be cleaned up along with his
environment if we are to do a "root and branch" job of reformation. Conversion is a true "transvaluation" in both personal and
social relations. A black theology must be *realistic* in reference
to its introspective concern in the black community and its
message of reconciliation aimed at overcoming the "polariza-
tion" between Blacks and Whites.

Sin is the deliberate choice of a lesser good, when a nobler
good is both *known* and *possible*. That is to say, in the face of
knowledge and freedom, one takes a lower road when a higher
moral clime is available. Man is, therefore, responsible for his
choice. Where there is freedom, there is concomitant responsi-

bility. Freedom is freedom *for,* not merely freedom *from.* This is a point to be made in black theology where freedom and power are so much prized. Another related consideration is that guilt is personal as well as social. We have been taught by the social and psychological theorists operating from positivistic and humanistic presuppositions that others are always at fault and the circumstances undergirding our actions explain (even criminal and immoral) behavior. According to the Christian faith there is personal guilt which accompanies every sinful free act. A black theology must be prophetic as well as priestly. The emphasis on sin must be matched by sanctifying grace. Grace, as God's unmerited favor, initiates conversion or the new birth and sustains Christian growth in the process of sanctification.

IV. Conclusion: Toward a Black Theology

What is our hope as black men? Is the promise of the future greater than the sufferings and disappointments of our past? If black theology is to be messianic, even eschatological, then, in what sense? The black Christian is born on the side of oppressed humanity and must have an understanding of his faith which commits him to the quest for freedom and justice in the contemporary struggle.

There is a great need to challenge the black intellectual, the group that E. Franklin Frazier called a "new middle class" or "black bourgeoisie." They have rejected the religion of childhood which will usually be Methodist or Baptist by denomination, but they have no philosophical substitute which is adequate to construct a world view that is meaningful. They will not embrace religious cults because they are mass-dominated. The Daddy Grace, Father Divine, and Black Muslim movements are usually unacceptable because of the large lower-class Negro membership. According to Frazier, when they decide that science doesn't have all the answers, they turn to faith healing and psychic phenomena. It has become a fad in cities to make a novena though they are not Catholics. They may even leave the church altogether and trust in "chance." Chance becomes a God-substitute.[2] If members of this new black middle class turn to religion, it is likely to be compartmentalized from all other

[2] E. Franklin Frazier, *Black Bourgeoisie* (New York: Collier, 1962), pp. 172–75.

aspects of life. Not all persons in this middle class are well-educated. Some are in this group by virtue of business success, political appointments, entertainment, sports, and the like. The religion of this class, where it does exist, is often a blind, anti-intellectual fundamentalism. It is a faith which they have been driven to, usually in middle life or old age, "by the ills that flesh is heir to." To use the language of the spirituals, they have arrived at this blind faith "by the troubles of this world."

The goal of black theology must somehow reach the "haves" among the Blacks who have deceived themselves into a social bankruptcy. According to Frazier, they have aimed at "nothingness" for their lives have been emptied of "both content and significance." [3] It is a fact that Frazier's analysis is alarmingly accurate and that a theology which speaks to the black experience must have the new middle class as well as the lower class of Blacks in view. A black theology must have as its goal the sociological and spiritual unity of the black community. To be the people of God, black Christians "must enter into covenant" with one another. The beloved community must be inclusive of black men and women from all stations in life. Pride in blackness must not only remove self-hate; it must erase the hatred, distrust, and tension that exist in the black community. Recently I had dinner with ten or twelve black students who were a "black caucus" on an integrated campus. Among several important concerns of the students was a desire to bring the black domestic servant into their caucus. They had found a "unity in blackness" which their parents had ignored, even rejected. Such a discovery deserves theological interpretation and must be an integral part of any black theology. Our common experience in blackness must issue into a deeper understanding of our oneness in Christ. A class and color conscious black church is a luxury which no black community can afford. We are one people both in nature and grace.

One black student who had done a great deal of serious reading in religious literature, but who was not yet convinced by the claims of Christianity, asked whether or not the Christian faith is against all forms of exclusiveness and if so, is it not

---

[3] Ibid., p. 195.

incompatible with black nationalism? A black theology cannot ignore this important issue. Our "getting together" as black Christians is to discover who we are. When we know our identity, have gained our self-respect, and are fully confident as a people, we will be in a position to be reconciled to others as equals and not as subordinates. If we can take our black consciousness up into our Christian faith, we will find it not only unmanly but unchristian to be reconciled on less than an equal basis. Our faith tells us that all are one in creation, sin, and redemption. As Christians we know that the practice of love is a two-way street and that the ties we have with the faithful lead us in and lead us out.

The ecumenical movement has taught us that as we seek a worldwide fellowship, we are driven to discover more clearly who we are as Baptists, Methodists, and so forth. The "black caucus" movement has created a "black ecumenism." We are seeking through these small fellowships to arrive at self-identification in order that we may know our past, our talents, our uniqueness as a people of God. In large integrated bodies we have been "mere faces in the crowd." We have been nameless, anonymous, culturally and historically disrobed, and religiously inhibited. We have not known ourselves; neither have we been free to be ourselves. The church, as the people of God, should be a fellowship in which everyone belongs—can be himself and do his own thing—"in the Lord" and under the direction of the Holy Spirit.

Finally, how hopeful is the theology of hope? Some who have been the most vocal advocates of a theology of revolution have not touched the racial crisis in the United States. I am highly suspicious when Paul Lehmann, who teaches on the fringe of the largest black ghetto in the world, can wax eloquent concerning a revolutionary theology which is his answer to the situation in Latin America. Surely a political theology to be meaningful must be applied to the local crisis situation. Prof. J. M. Lochman, from Prague, has "cultivated his own garden" as Voltaire would phrase it. Lochman has applied his insights to the Christian-Marxist dialogue in a communist land. Another American, Prof. Richard Shaull of Princeton Seminary, has spoken on "Revolutionary Change in Theological Perspec-

tive," but he, too, has selected Latin America. A black theologian, aware of the sufferings of his people (for in various
ways he suffers together with his family, with his black brothers) has the responsibility to speak *first* to the American situation.

At the Duke Conference on the Theology of Hope, I put the
question to Moltmann, the arch-advocate of the theology of
hope, as to the meaning of his theology for an oppressed people.
His answer at that time was not very hopeful. To his credit,
however, he has come out most recently with a very forthright
application of this theological position on the side of the oppressed.[4] Martin Luther King, Jr. was assassinated the very
night that Moltmann delivered his position paper. The next
morning, with this tragedy weighing heavily upon my mind, I
raised the above question regarding the relevance of the theology of hope for the racial crisis. In this more recent statement, Moltmann makes reference to Dr. King as follows:

> Martin Luther King took the side of the blacks and the
> poor. He organized strikes and protest marches against white
> racism and the capitalist society in his country. Yet he always
> had the arrogance and fear of the whites in mind—their lack
> of salvation. He mobilized the blacks and the poor not only to
> revenge the blacks against the whites, but also to redeem both
> black and white from racial alienation.[5]

Moltmann adds: "The human revolution is not out to turn the
slaves into masters but to get rid of the whole wretched master-
slave structure, so that men may be able to treat one another
as men." [6]

A very close admirer of Moltmann, Frederick Herzog, writing in *The Journal of Religious Thought*, has asserted that theology should become revolutionary in this time of global crisis.
Like Moltmann he is impressed with King's "nonviolent revolution." It goes without saying that a black theology must be a
political theology in the sense that it will challenge the structures of power and seek the humanization of all institutions.

I have some personal reservations about the theology of
hope. Any theological outlook requires some "indigenization"

[4] Jürgen Moltmann, "God in the Revolution," *The Student World*, Vol.
LXI, No. 3, pp. 241–52.
[5] Ibid., p. 247.
[6] Ibid.

before it is suitable as a formulation of the Christian understanding of the black experience. Moltmann's theology is a theology of the word centering in eschatology rather than Christology. His view of revelation is too narrow for the openness that is desirable. Eschatology focuses on the future and lifts up the theme of hope, but it must, for my part, be "a realizable eschatology" in the here and now in order to be hopeful to black Christians. The theme of the "waiting God" is unacceptable for those who have been waiting so long and who are tired of waiting. This is bad psychology—even if it turns out to be good theology. The "I am of God" is more impressive than the "I will be of God." "Will be" is part of the duration of the life of an eternal God. We need to affirm the "isness" of the "wasness" as well. God who was our help in ages past is also our hope for years to come.

A black theology must combine the "inner felt" and the "outer known." We must combine our subjective experience with objective knowledge. Among the existent creative theological movements, the theology of hope may be the most satisfying in forging a constructive theological statement of the black experience. The theme of hope for an oppressed people is exhilarating and political theology which places Christian faith firmly on the side of the disinherited with equality and reconciliation as its goal, is attractive. Though this has been a position paper, it is nevertheless exploratory in character. Therefore, in sum, the end is only the beginning. A statement by Herzog in his essay "God, Evil, and Revolution," seems to say well what I would like to stress in my final words:

> Revolutionary change seems a real possibility offered us to arrive at a better use of power. On the one hand, the Christian is compelled to stand at a critical distance from man's revolution so that he will not identify the tentative and relative of revolutions with absolute goodness. On the other hand, he is constrained, in this attitude of critical distance, to the deepest involvement in revolutionary change, since only here can he find the concrete foretaste of God's coming Kingdom in which God will make all things new.[7]

[7] Frederick Herzog, "God, Evil, and Revolution," *The Journal of Religious Thought*, Vol. XXV, No. 2, 1968–69, pp. 27–28.

# Chapter Five

# THE ETHICS OF BLACK POWER

*Preston N. Williams*

"Without rebellion, mankind would stagnate, and injustice would be irremediable. The man who refuses to obey authority has, therefore, in certain circumstances, a legitimate function, provided his disobedience has motives which are social rather than personal." [1]

This quotation from Bertrand Russell provides us with a suitable place of beginning. It suggests that rebellion is sometimes called forth by injustice and that some of those who rebel are motivated by social considerations. The ethical aspects of the black church/black theology phenomenon are certainly related to both these motifs.

The black church/black theology movement exists because of the past, present, and continuing desire of white Christians to deny that the black man is a child of God. Ninety percent of black Christians are outside the white church not because of their lack of a coherent theological system but simply because they are black. In America at least the ecumenical movement does not include all the body of Christ because to do so would be to accept what Americans call miscegenation.

The first ethical aspect of the black church phenomenon then is its willingness to make plain the actual state of relationships among white and black Christians. We are separated brethren. No amount of special departments—social justice or church and race—no number of national and international conferences on race presided over by white Americans of distinction; no enumeration of white persons who have given their

[1] Bertrand Russell, *Power: A New Social Analysis* (New York: Barnes & Noble, 1962), p. 171.

life in service to the Negro; no counting of the good deeds performed by this or that klatch of white Christians can obscure this fact. White Christians and black Christians in America have been and are separated brethren. The black church and black theology phenomenon simply makes us aware of the obvious.

James Luther Adams, in an article describing the emergence of the black Unitarian and Universalist caucus, describes this new awareness as a "shock of recognition": a moment in which some white Christians and some black Christians come to recognize that reality is not as they have pictured it, that their attitude needs to be reversed, and that the situation in which the church finds itself needs to be changed. This ethical insight is the fruit of the black church/black theology phenomenon.

Many no doubt rue the day when the black church took this posture. The black church, many felt, should have turned its back upon Black Power and added its weight to those condemning the new more militant slogan of the black community. Yet to have done so would have been to turn against the imperative need for massive social change both in order to implement what was already legislated and to root out what grave evil remained. To have condemned Black Power would have involved the black church in the substitution of symptom for cause, which was and still is the strategy of so much of the nation and the church today. The cause of the malaise we were to be told much later was white racism. The black church/black theology phenomenon anticipated that event by a year (July 27, 1967) and declared on July 31, 1966 what was the root of America's dilemma. "We are faced now with a situation where conscienceless power meets powerless conscience, threatening the very foundation of our nation." [2]

An adequate ethic must operate at two levels: that of the social and that of the personal. There must be both a disciplining of power and of conscience. The National Committee of Negro Churchmen sought in their statement to pinpoint both these matters, to suggest how "the shock of recognition" should

---

[2] "Black Power" Statement by National Committee of Negro Churchmen, *The New York Times*, July 31, 1966.

affect every aspect of the existence of the black and the white man.

The ethical consequences for personal behavior are the most clearly focused aspect of the Negro's new awareness of his blackness. Let us begin by sketching the outline of the personal dimension of ethics. Perhaps the words that capture best the new consciousness are "soul" and "self-determination."

Soul, of course, is a very elusive word and no definition of it will prove to be adequate, I am sure. It appears to me, however, that this is the very reason why the concept is so crucial to the new black man. What he is saying is that the very springs of action and motivation in the Negro are conditioned in a manner different from that of the white man. The difference in the final analysis is not asserted to be racial but cultural and historical. It is due to the long years of suffering and bondage, of hunger and poverty, of living at life's edge and finding in the heart of one's misery a reason for keeping on. Despite the propaganda of other ethnic groups the black man knows his sorrow to be unique and from that uniqueness he asserts has sprung an attitude toward life that permeates his total existence.

If I may paraphrase DuBois, I think I can express my belief and I hope that of the black man about soul. Soul is the constant feeling of one's two-ness, of being a part yet not being a part. It is the warring of two thoughts, two ideals, two unreconciled strivings within one dark body. Soul is the expression of both the black man's freedom and his bondage. It is a spontaneous and free response to life, yet also the stolid, stoical response to a fate one can barely endure and from which one can never fully escape. Soul catches up both the heroism and the pathos of black life, its frenzies of joy and its dark sullen sorrow.

Soul is elusive and vague, it is contradictory and confusing: it is the heart and marrow of black existence. When then the black church/black theology phenomenon gave expression to soul it was affirming the black man's right to be himself.

The need for the illumination of the ethical by the historical, the universal by the particular, the abstract by the concrete, the principle by the context had already proceeded a great distance in Christian ethics. H. Richard Niebuhr had given a lifetime to this type of ethical endeavor, and the popularity of Bonhoeffer and the contextualist modes of thought made this new insight an indispensable tool for the Christian ethicist. Nevertheless few if any moralists had employed the device to analyze the problem of race relations. Following the lead of Martin Luther King, race relations were always deductively arrived at from an analysis of sacrificial love and nonviolence. The black man remained thus an abstraction despite the fact that at every stage of King's crusades one was made increasingly aware of the peculiar history and tradition of the black man in America and the peculiar stamp that history made upon his character. Every success of King contributed to the black man's increasing need for being himself. Finally from the frustrations of youth and also from their impetuousness came the catalyst that was to force the new awareness to surface. Out of the dark bowels of the South; out of the black belt in which the black man had suffered most, been crushed, defeated, and killed; out of Mississippi came the cry of liberation, Black Power! Black Power!

Fortunately black churchmen heard the cry. They perceived both the legitimacy of its demand for a more adequate social and cultural base for protest and its need to be conditioned by the historical insights regarding power and goodness contained in the Christian faith. Their aphorism concerning conscienceless power and powerless conscience plus their continuing activities have been an attempt to speak to both issues. There have been some hits and some misses but their instincts have been correct.

That instinct has been the desire to find a Christian perspective for the black experience in America and its rootage in Africa. The Christian faith was to be adapted in such a way as to provide an interpretation of the soul of black folks, to catch the two-ness of the black man.

The history of modern Christianity has been largely apologetic. It has been an attempt to indicate what useful insights and correctives the Christian faith is able to provide for the understanding of science, of technology, and of the many new forms of human living. Insofar as the black man has not fully shared in this concern for relevance because of his peculiar social, economic, and racial plight, Christian spokesmen have had no Word of God to address to him. Nor did a philosophy of the trickle-down dissemination of truth function adequately. The black man was simply left out of the concerns of Christian apologetics as it became increasingly more relevant, more avant-garde, more elitist.

The exception to this type of development was the much celebrated missions to the inner city. Through these endeavors the church strove to fulfill its responsibility to the lower classes, many of whom were black. Any fairminded evaluation of this work will reveal, however, that despite the publicity, its impact was relatively slight. Moreover, when one looks into the work which was performed, one sees, until the very recent past, no concern for or appreciation of the religious background of the peoples of the inner city and no development of relationships with the black churches of the ghetto. Black religion was to be upgraded; that is, made to conform to mainstream white Christianity and the models had more of a relationship to Greenwich Village than Harlem or Georgia. Soul was neither understood nor valued. Inadvertently men who possessed a real concern for black personality and community were engaged in the enterprise of cultivating among Blacks a disrespect for their past and their religious heritage.

The black church/black theology phenomenon seeks to reverse this. It seeks to see the black man as rooted in community; the black community, the community of oppressed people, the American community, the African community, the Christian community. To all these the black man has a loyalty. To only one of these is the loyalty an ultimate one, but until the ethnic loyalties are more seriously considered by religionists the black man's life will be twisted and distorted and his perception of God skewed.

Powerless conscience tells the story of a man, a race that has been asked to fulfill the highest values of Western Christian ethic, while being denied the power to be himself. Only by a recovery of his historical existence, only by a rooting of the *ought* in the *is* can powerless conscience become powerful conscience. It is in this direction that black theology moves.

Being may be more fundamental than doing but doing is

of grave importance. The new black church/black theology movement does not, therefore, ignore doing. Soul thus is more than "a metaphorical evocation of Negro being as expressed in the Negro tradition." [3] It is a way of life even if not always a Christian style of life. Black theology is well aware of this. The Black Power Statement of 1966 therefore states: "We commit ourselves as churchmen to make more meaningful in the life of our institution our conviction that Jesus Christ reigns in the 'here' and 'now' as well as in the future he brings in upon us." [4]

Black theology does seek to be Christian theology despite the assertions of some of its critics. It is seeking not simply to provide a framework of meaning for black experience, but it is seeking to transform black life so that it more closely resembles the life of the Christ. Because, however, black theology emerges from the life of the black man in American society and in Western Christianity, it finds it necessary to apprise the black man of his Christian responsibility to be a disruptive force in a racist society and a racist church. The black man must on occasion refuse to obey authority in order that he may fulfill God's vocation for the black man and God's will for our time. While Protestants and Catholics plan for unity, the black church must plan for disunity.

One of the clichés that abounds in contemporary Christianity is "making human life more human." Prior to this we spoke of accepting our acceptance and, in the midst of this desire to make possible the emergence of a mature, authentic person, we stressed as never before the significance of data and context in ethical decision-making. While the church has been reluctant to apply any of this new teaching to groups other than the white middle class and the secular humanist, the black church has taken upon itself the task of making black life more human, of getting black people to accept their acceptance, and of helping to bring into existence mature, authentic black persons. The task is neither pleasant nor in the usual sense profitable. It is truly a work performed for the greater glory of God and for the renewal of true piety in the church. In one sense the

---

[3] Lerone Bennett, Jr., *The Negro Mood and Other Essays* (Chicago: Johnson Publishing Co., 1964), p. 89.
[4] "Black Power" Statement, *op. cit.*, Part III.

mission is not relevant. It does not relate directly to COCU, the population explosion, medical ethics, or even nuclear and other forms of war. As journalistic theology and churchmanship, black theology comes off rather poorly. There can be only one motivation for this type of activity, namely Jesus' concern to make all men whole and his desire to accept men as historical beings. Christianity cannot rob the black man of his blackness unless it desires him to be something less than a man. The black church and black theology thus seeks to permit the black man to be both black and Christian.

Black theology suggests therefore that human life can become more human only when men are permitted to accept their own humanity. Not the humanity of the catacombs or the Middle Ages, not the humanity of Geneva or Worms, not the humanity of seventeenth-century England or of seventeenth-century America but the humanity that is the legacy of slavery, of victimization and discrimination in America. The humanity which is the result of one's black skin and kinky hair, of one's violation by white persons and institutions, and of one's life in a ghetto. How does one accept the unacceptable and at the same time proceed in the direction of reconciliation with the oppressor? How does one love the enemy? How does one start with the isness of life, the situation, and proceed to godliness? This is the task the black church and black theology has accepted and it is an ethical task of no mean proportion.

Certainly success shall mean a redefinition of soul and a reinterpretation of the Christian heritage. One would assume that an open church and a servant church would lend this enterprise every assistance and yet such is not the case. Catholic must still be qualified by Roman, and World Council by Reformed and Orthodox. Particularities can everywhere be seen as bearers of the universals except, that is, in relation to the black man. Then and only then particularities frustrate community and kill brotherhood. At least that is what black men are told. Black theology is convinced that not only white men but black men also can speak their own tongue and that the God who is above all can make possible the miracle of the one church. Now that we know by means of the shock of recognition who we are and from whence we have come, we can seek to make our mutual Christian faith inclusive of the black experience and we can make the black experience the bearer of Christian values. This is the ethical message as regards the person that flows out from the black church and black theology. To the extent that we can appropriate it, we can make both black and white men whole and we can bring unity and strength to Christ's church. The Black Power Statement puts it a little differently: "If the future is to belong to any of us, it must be prepared for all of us whatever our racial or religious background. For in the final analysis, we are *persons* and the power of all groups must be wielded to make visible our common humanity." [5]

I have stated previously the fact that ethics exists at two levels: the personal and the social. In life and in the black churchmen's statement, these levels are intertwined. Separation of the two is absolutely essential, however, because of the truth stated long ago by Reinhold Niebuhr.

> Our contemporory culture fails to realise the power, extent and persistence of group egoism in human relations. It may be possible, though it is never easy, to establish just relations between individuals within a group purely by moral and rational suasion and accommodation. In inter-group relations this is practically an impossibility. The relations between groups must therefore always be predominantly political rather than ethical, that is, they will be determined by the proportion of power which each group possesses at least as much as by any rational and moral appraisal of the comparative needs and claims of each group. The coercive factors, in distinction to the more purely moral and rational factors, in political relations can never be sharply differentiated and defined.[6]

Relations between Blacks and Whites are not simply relations among individuals. They are relations among groups and as such involve coercion, force, and social conflict. Love and goodwill must be present but alone they cannot do the job. A social ethic thus will always have present in it political as well as ethical considerations. Nevertheless a social ethic seeks to create a good society and this means that good must reside

5 Ibid.
6 Reinhold Niebuhr, *Moral Man and Immoral Society* (New York: Charles Scribner's Sons, 1932), pp. xxii–xxiii.

not only in isolated individuals but in institutions and in organizations of men. Without these good institutions and good organizations there can be no good race relations.

The black church/black theology phenomenon seeks to take account of these facts. Powerless conscience is conjoined to conscienceless power. The black person is described as one who must fight desperately in order to win and preserve his manhood; the white man is described as a member of a majority group that wields conscienceless power. Conscienceless because there is an element of hypocrisy involved in the claim of Whites that black separatist groups impede integration. Conscienceless because Whites employ all the means of law, coercion, economic control, power to impose their will upon Blacks and yet contend that Blacks can only legitimately use persuasion and reason. Conscienceless because the advantages enjoyed by Whites are always described as the product of achievement and merit when much of it is due to the special privileges accorded their white skin.

The insensitivity of the white majority concerning its usage of power is sharply outlined by the black churchmen, not for the purpose of being disagreeable or uncooperative but rather in an effort to introduce honesty into the discussion of reconciliation. The insensitivity, the black churchmen remind us, cannot be equated with a breach of etiquette, nor can it be attributed alone to white conservatives or bigots. It is the insensitivity of white liberals and moderates, of the white poor and the white disadvantaged. In a measure all Whites benefit from white conscienceless power and all Blacks are victimized. Conscienceless power is the expression of a group; in its benefits and its damage all Whites participate.

There has been so much venting of hostile feelings against Whites by Blacks that we might ask what is the ethical value of this type of activity. What purpose does it serve? Reinhold Niebuhr's words are still meaningful: "Only the proletarian sees how the centralisation of power and privilege in modern society proceeds so rapidly that it not only outrages the conscience but destroys the very foundations of society." [7]

---

[7] Ibid., p. 165.

The role of the prophet in modern society is peculiarly that of the black man and the black church. Black theology and the black church is the proper critic, not of the individual sins of white individuals but of the collective sins that Whites have consciously or unconsciously built into the structures of their society, their churches, and their other institutions. The criticism, therefore, of Whites is primarily a criticism not of individuals but of them as a class or a group; a group which possesses great power, wealth, and affluence but which refuses to allocate its resources in such a way as to serve the real well-being of the bottom third of the American society.

It is interesting that the white majority has so easily accepted the view that domestic reform is too expensive or upsetting, that international commitments deserve a higher priority than those made to the black man at home. It is interesting to note how cabinet members, senators, legislators, the President can threaten prosecution of black students for self-segregation and black persons for militancy and yet sanction and reward the continual disregard of national law and human justice when the black man is concerned. Against this the black church/black theology phenomenon must and does protest. Protest because it sees white liberals and conservatives joined in an open conspiracy to keep the black man in his place. Protest because it sees daily the human products of domestic economy, lack of commitment to racial justice, and duplicity in government. Protest because it lives with those who cannot escape because their skin and hair say who they are no matter what else they may acquire or possess.

The criticism by the black churchman is a criticism of society, not primarily individuals. As a consequence the changes they demand are institutional changes; a renewal of society and a renewal of the church. What is demanded is a restructuring of the relationship between groups and a reallocation of the power resources possessed by communities and institutions. A reordering of public school control systems and educational programs, a revision of college admission procedures and curriculums, a revival of poverty programs and job training, an adequate provision for welfare services and health care; these are programs that enhance the common good and ensure a minimum quality of life for all persons. Upon them can be built the foundation of a more reasonable and sympathetic social order. As Bertrand Russell suggests, black churchmen are in the peculiar position of being able to call for reform, to be disobedient for motives that are social rather than personal. While I cannot equate the black church or black churchmen with either the role of suffering servant or chosen people, I have no doubt but that any meaningful change must of necessity incorporate the goals and objectives, the motifs and content, the participation and involvement of black men, black organizations, and black institutions. This is inevitable if we are to seek justice, for the black man sees and analyzes—at this time in history—the pretensions of white America and white Christianity.

Let me remind you that Christian social ethics is not simply speculation about the future state of society or the problems and concerns of the powerful and privileged groups of society. It is also critical reflection upon the past with an eye toward correcting the sins of the present. The concerns of all the children of God are to be addressed. While not being disqualified for the first, the black church is especially well fitted to perform the second and crucially important task.

The black church's adoption of this role as social critic is a venture in risk-taking of the highest order. Long considered as invisible or inferior, it now opens itself to the charge of being racist and heretical. The current refusal of the Roman Catholic Church to be supportive of social change means that the black priest and nuns open themselves to the gravest penalties for disrespect of authority. The failure of the Protestant churches to make black-white reconciliation more imperative than ecumenical mergers or avant-garde experimentation means that black caucuses risk bad publicity, token funding, and complete ostracism from church decision-making. Conscienceless power is more pervasive in the church than in society because churchmen are more convinced than others of their high morality and their good practices. The black church is out on a limb and it will have to validate its criticism in the presence of a disbelieving and fearful foe.

It behooves us then to know exactly what the black church

is requesting in order that we may judge fairly its criticism. A single line from the Black Power Statement set forth the request. The churchmen seek "equal opportunity *in life* as well as *in law*." [8] The force of this pithy line should not be lost upon us. It is an attack not only upon our conception of the equal protection of the law but also upon our conception of achievement and merit, the systems by which groups and persons acquire power. What is asserted is that Whites possess power and privilege not always because of justice but quite often because of the privilege provided by their white skins. Administrative posts in denominations, deanships of theological seminaries, pastorates in churches are awarded more on skin color than ability. As in the church so also in the society, injustice and discrimination mock our claim to achievement and merit as the primary criteria of choice. The black churchmen challenge, therefore, the moral and Christian legitimation of many of our present laws, practices, and conceptions of due process. The black churchmen seek, therefore, to make the system work justly, to achieve authentic democracy in the society and true Christianity in the church. Power for the black man is sought not by robbing others of their proper rights but by requiring that social institutions—the police, government, economy, church, and other social institutions—function according to the ethical norms of justice and equality. Despite the cry of revolution the goal is the well-being of all persons and the realization of the good society. The present manner in which power is utilized is being challenged because power must be used equitably and for good if there is to be integrity in personal and social relations and justice and love in society.

Equal opportunity in life as well as in law also suggests that the good society cannot be wholly constructed of law. Life is bigger than law. Power includes love and must be employed with conscience. Reconciliation must include a mutual sharing of the resources that make for equality in living. If white Christians can come to accept a black Messiah the tendency to make their skin color the object of worship may receive a fatal blow. Perhaps then they can see the black man as a Christian brother

8 "Black Power" Statement, *op. cit.*, Part I.

and recognize that humanly conditioned symbols cannot be equated with ultimate reality. At the same time that the black Messiah serves to unmask conscienceless White Power it will serve to give power to the conscience of the black man and make him realize more fully his Christian ethical indicative.

Obviously I am making another assertion, also, setting forth another belief; namely, that the more universal rendition of Christian symbols will be undertaken, even as the black churchmen contend, with the aim of making "more meaningful in the life of our institution our conviction that Jesus Christ reigns in the 'here' and 'now' as well as in the future he brings in upon us." [9] The same concern of the black churchmen is expressed in the churchmen's advice to the mass media. Here it is stated in secular language. "Nothing is now more important than that you look for a variety of sources of truth in order that the limited perspectives of all of us might be corrected." [10] The white Christ and white Christianity is a limited perspective. So, too, the black Christ and black Christianity. Black and white both shall need a correction of their limited perspective. I think that can come if we accept in proper spirit the words of the black churchmen.

I have tried to sketch in brief outline some of the implications for social ethics that are present in the Black Power Statement of the National Committee of Negro (Black) Churchmen. The most germane ethical implication of the document is set forth in their declaration on the Urban Mission. In that document the churchmen state:

> We believe it would be a tragic mistake for predominately white denominations to choose to by-pass this institution [the black church] in an effort to relate to and invest in the urban ghettoes. The black church has a physical presence and a constituency already organized in these communities. It is available as a means by which the whole Christian community can deal substantively and effectively with the urban crisis, the sickness of body and spirit which we see in the metropolitan centers of America today.

In the age of COCU and in the age of social conflict among the races, this statement of black churchmen raises a serious ethical problem for Christianity. Can the white church in its

9 Ibid., Part III.
10 Ibid., Part IV.

task of restructuring itself take seriously the black church? Can it combine departments of church and race and urban ministry into one? Can it restructure its urban ministry in such a way as to make it part of the black church? If the white church takes seriously the black church it should seek to establish a working relationship with its black Christian brothers who live and work in the ghetto. It should seek the wisdom of the black church and seek to strengthen the black church. The magazine *Church in Metropolis* ought to be run in cooperation with—if not solely by—the black caucuses of the white denominations who sponsor and subsidize it. One gets little impression of the white church's belief in reconciliation while reading a white sheet from the white church with but one or two carefully placed articles by black men.

I think I know all the counterarguments used by the white church to defend its policies. We were there first. Were you really? We are more able. Why then have you had so little effect on either white or black Christians or the society? It's our money! Are we speaking now of conscienceless power? If the white church and white Christianity are seriously interested in the black church and are not simply concerned to assuage their own guilt or accumulate merit points in suburbia, they will begin now to confer with black churchmen about the transfer of power, resources, money to the black church. Such an action may be just the catalyst we are seeking in order to put COCU once again on the move and to provide a national model for the next stage in racial reconciliation. I am confident that such a magnanimous but also just and Christian act would do much more than anything else we can presently imagine to bring white and black Christians together. There would be, to quote the black churchmen, a "renewal and enhancement of the black church in terms of its liturgical life, its theological interpretation, its understanding of its mission to itself, to the white church and to the nation." [11] Moreover, this is a process all of us are close enough to to influence. Black churchmen seek a unity which is not another version of patronizing missions. To bring this unity to pass white churchmen must rid them-

[11] Statement of the National Committee of Black Churchmen on the Urban Mission in a Time of Crisis, p. 2.

selves of conscienceless power and adopt in earnest a more Christian concept of stewardship.

The ethical implications of Black Power as understood and defined by the black churchmen are quite numerous and potentially Christian. I hope I have outlined a few of the more important ones. In the area of personal ethics the churchmen seek to make it possible for wholesome black family existence and proper personal development for every man, woman, and child. In a society and a Christian community that takes seriously both family and the individual, this should be an easy task. History and the daily acts of white citizens and churchmen suggest that the evaluation of family and person will not readily be extended to the black man. The churchmen's task will thus be fraught with great difficulty. The soft gentle voices of greed seem determined to keep the black man in a state of dependency and childhood.

They also seek to keep for themselves the affluence and wealth of America and of the church. The black churchmen seek a redistribution of this power because they desire to see a new quality of church life and social existence. They seek a whole church in a healthy and sane world.

# Chapter Six

# JESUS, THE LIBERATOR

*Joseph A. Johnson, Jr.*

Paul, in 1 Corinthians 1:18–24, speaks about the doctrine of the cross. To some, this doctrine is sheer folly; to others, it is the power of God. Some thought the doctrine of the cross was weakness, but to the believers it is a revelation of the power of God, the wisdom of God, and the love of God. Jesus Christ is the subject of the gospel. Paul writes:

> The doctrine of the cross is sheer folly to those on their way to ruin, but to us who are on the way to salvation it is the power of God. Scripture says, "I will destroy the wisdom of the wise, and bring to nothing the cleverness of the clever." Where is your wise man now, your man of learning, or your subtle debater—limited, all of them, to this passing age? God has made the wisdom of this world look foolish. As God in his wisdom ordained, the world failed to find him by its wisdom, and he chose to save those who have faith by the folly of the Gospel. Jews call for miracles, Greeks look for wisdom; but we proclaim Christ—yes, Christ nailed to the cross; and though this is a stumbling-block to Jews and folly to Greeks, yet to those who have heard his call, Jews and Greeks alike, he is the power of God and the wisdom of God (NEB).[1]

Jesus, the Liberator, is the power of God, the wisdom of God, and the love of God. Paul knew firsthand of the operation of these qualities, wisdom, power, and love. He could never quite understand this new wisdom, this new power, and this new love which he had experienced in Jesus, the Liberator. It was a queer kind of wisdom and love that had chosen him, one who had been a persecutor of the church and now summoned to be a messenger of the crucified-risen Lord. He could never

---

[1] From *The New English Bible, New Testament.* © The Delegates of the Oxford University Press and the Syndics of the Cambridge University Press 1961. Reprinted by permission.

comprehend this kind of love that had permitted Jesus, God's only son, to die on the cross for the salvation of men. Paul is astonished and amazed at this new revelation of love: "While we were yet helpless, at the right time Christ died for the ungodly. Why, one will hardly die for a righteous man—though perhaps for a good man one will dare even to die. But God shows his love for us in that while we were yet sinners Christ died for us (Rom. 5:6–8)."

Paul's new life had been determined by this encounter with Jesus, the Liberator. This new life which was God-given was the life of grace, and he shouts, "By the grace of God, I am what I am." The experience of this wisdom, power, and love, Paul defines as "the power of God unto salvation." It was a new kind of power, a power that had granted him freedom to life, righteousness, peace, and joy, and also freedom from sin, from the law, and from death. The liberating power of Jesus had emancipated him and set him free. He exhorts his fellow Christians: "For freedom Christ has set us free; stand fast therefore, and do not submit again to a yoke of slavery (Gal. 5:1)."

Jesus, the Liberator, had given to Paul not only freedom but also a new self-understanding. This new self-understanding, according to Bultmann, is bestowed with faith and it is freedom through which the believer gains life and thereby his own self.[2] Paul discovered that he who belongs to Jesus, the Liberator, and thus to God, has become master of everything. He declares to the Christians at Corinth that this grace-freedom event which they had experienced in Jesus, the Liberator, placed the whole world at their disposal: "So let no one boast of men. For all things are yours, whether Paul or Apollos or Cephas or the world or life or death or the present or the future, all are yours; and you are Christ's; and Christ is God's (1 Cor. 3:21–23)."

Jesus is the Liberator. He is the revelation of the wisdom, the power, and the love of God. This was the message which the early Christian preachers were commissioned to proclaim. This message was called the Kerygma. We preach Christ, Paul shouts. At the heart of the Kerygma lies this fundamental

---

[2] Rudolph Bultmann, *Theology of the New Testament*, tr. Kendrick Grobel, Vol. I (London: SCM Press, 1952), pp. 330–31.

christological affirmation: Jesus is the Liberator! Jesus is the Emancipator!

Nineteen hundred years have passed since these stirring words were written by Paul and various interpretations of Jesus, the Liberator, have been presented. These interpretations range all the way from Jesus as the Son of God, of Paul, the writers of the Synoptic Gospels, John and Hebrews to the Jesus of Barth, Brunner, Bonhoeffer, Tillich, and Kierkegaard.

The tragedy of the interpretations of Jesus by the white American theologians during the last three hundred years is that Jesus has been too often identified with the oppressive structures and forces of the prevailing society. His teachings have been used to justify wars, exploitation of the poor and oppressed peoples of the world. In his name the most vicious form of racism has been condoned and advocated. In a more tragic sense this Jesus of the white church establishment has been white, straight-haired, blue-eyed, Anglo-Saxon; that is, presented in the image of the oppressor. This "whiteness" has prevailed to the extent that the black, brown, or red peoples of the world, who had accepted Jesus as Lord and Savior, were denied full Christian fellowship in his church and were not accepted as brothers for whom Jesus died.

I have been asked to address myself to the theme, "The Christian Faith in a Revolutionary Age" and to indicate the techniques by which this faith may be communicated. You should expect that we would first critically evaluate the existing understanding of the Christian faith as interpreted and presented by white theologians and as a black American reveal to you the thinking concerning this interpretation of the Christian faith in the black community. We begin with the premise that white theology is severely limited in its interpretation of the Christian faith insofar as the nonwhite peoples of the world are concerned. This limitation is one of the causes for the quest for a black Messiah.

## THE LIMITATIONS OF WHITE THEOLOGY

To be sure, during the past fifteen years we have entered, insofar as the black community is concerned, into one of the most exciting periods in the life of the black people of this country. For more than one hundred years black students have studied in predominantly white seminaries and have been served a theological diet, created, mixed, and dosed out by white theological technicians. The black seminarians took both the theological milk and meat and even when they had consumed these, their souls were still empty. Those of us who went through the white seminaries did not understand why then. We had passed the courses in the four major fields of studies; we knew our Barth, Brunner, and Niebuhr. We had entered deeply into a serious study of Bonhoeffer and Tillich, but we discovered that these white theologians had described the substance and had elucidated a contemporary faith for the white man. These white scholars knew nothing about the black experience, and to many of them this black experience was illegitimate and unauthentic.

The black man's religious style was considered subhuman by many of the white theological seminaries of this nation and the emotional nature of his religious experience was termed primitive. For the black seminary student to become a great preacher really meant that he had to *whitenize* himself. He had to suppress his naturalness and remake himself in the image of a Sockman, Fosdick, or Buttrick. You see, insofar as the white seminaries were concerned there were no great black preachers, and if a black preacher was fortunate to be called great by the white community, it meant that he was merely a pale reflection of the white ideal.

The young black seminary student today has been introduced into a whole new experience—one fashioned by the late Martin Luther King, Jr. but clarified and profoundly interpreted by Frantz Fanon, Malcolm X, Stokely Carmichael, and Ron Karenga. The young black seminary student today has been tried by every conceivable ordeal that sadistic racial minds can devise; from the fire hoses to vicious dogs, from tear gas to electric animal prods. They have matched wits with the white racist of the power structure and are helping to pull down the system of segregation and discrimination. They have no objection to the combination of such words "black and power," "black and theology," "black and church," "black and Christ," "black and God." They believe DuBois who wrote, "This assumption that of all the hues of God, whiteness is inherently and obviously better than brownness or tan leads to curious acts." They are not shocked, nor are they discouraged if the term Black Power seems to offend or frighten white or black Americans. To these young Blacks, Black Power means consciousness and solidarity. It means the amassing by black people of the economic, political, and judicial control necessary to define their own goals and share in the decisions that determine their faith. Fanon, Malcolm X, Carmichael, and Karenga forced the black seminary students to ask these questions: What do these white American and European theologians of a white-racist-dominated religious establishment know about the soul of black folks? What do Barth, Brunner, and Tillich know about the realities of the black ghettos or the fate of black sharecroppers' families whose souls are crushed by the powerful forces of a society that considers everything black as evil? Could these white theologians see the image of the crucified Jesus in the mutilated face of a rat-bitten child, or a drug addict, bleeding to death in a stinking alley?

We have learned that the interpretation of Christian theology and of Jesus expounded by white American theologians is severely limited. This is due to the simple reason that these white scholars have never been lowered into the murky depth of the black experience of reality. They never conceived the black Jesus walking the dark streets of the ghettos of the North and the sharecropper's farm in the Deep South without a job, busted, and emasculated. These white theologians could never hear the voice of Jesus speaking in the dialect of Blacks from the southern farms, or in the idiom of the Blacks of the ghetto. This severe limitation of the white theologians' inability to articulate the full meaning of the Christian faith has given rise to the development of black theology.

The Commission on Theology of the National Committee of Black Churchmen has issued a statement on black theology. In this document black theology is defined:

> For us, Black theology is the theology of black liberation. It seeks to plumb the black condition in the light of God's revelation in Jesus Christ, so that the black community can see the gospel is commensurate with the achievement of black humanity. Black Theology is a theology of "blackness." It is the af-

firmation of black humanity that emancipates black people from white racism thus providing authentic freedom for both white and black people. It affirms the humanity of white people in that it says "No" to the encroachment of white oppression.[3]

The black scholars are indebted in a measure to white theologians. We have learned much from them. However, the white theologians in their interpretation of the Christian faith have ignored the black Christian experience. Many have felt that this black Christian experience was devoid of meaning and therefore could be omitted in their exposition and interpretation of the Christian faith. To be sure, this was a grievous error. The omission of the black Christian experience by white interpreters of the Christian faith meant that the message of the Christian faith thus interpreted was oriented toward the white community. Therefore this message had nothing significant to say to the black man who is now struggling for identity and dignity. The black theologians were forced to look at the black Christian experience and interpret this experience so as to ascertain what the black Christian experience has to say to the black man concerning the vital matters of the Christian faith. Black theology is a product of black Christian experience and reflection. It comes out of the past. It is strong in the present and we believe it is redemptive for the future.

## THE QUEST FOR THE BLACK JESUS

The reason for the quest for the black Jesus is deeply embedded in the black man's experience in this country. The black man's introduction to the white Jesus was a catastrophe! Vincent Harding reminds us that the Blacks encountered the American white Christ first on the slave ships that brought us to these shores. The Blacks on the slave ship heard his name sung in hymns of praise while they died chained in stinky holes beneath the decks locked in terror and disease. When the Blacks leaped from the decks of the slave ships they saw his name carved on the side of the ship. When the black women were raped in the cabin by the white racists, they must have noticed the Holy

---

[3] "Black Theology: A Statement of the National Committee of Black Churchmen," June 13, 1969.

Bible on the shelves. Vincent Harding declares, "The horrors continued on American soil. So all through the nation's history many black men have rejected this Christ—indeed the miracle is that so many accepted him. In past times our disdain often had to be stifled and sullen, our angers silent and self-destructive. But now we speak out." [4]

One white perceptive theologian, Kyle Haselden, has observed:

> The white man cleaves Christian piety into two parts: the strong, virile virtues he applies exclusively to himself; the apparently weak, passive virtues he endorses especially for the Negro. "Whatsoever things are true, honest, just, pure, lovely" belong to the white man; "whatsoever things are of good report" belong to the Negro. The white man takes the active and positive Christian adjectives for himself: noble, manly, wise, strong, courageous; he recommends the passive and negative Christian adjectives to the Negro: patient, long-suffering, humble, self-effacing, considerate, submissive, childlike, meek. [5]

White theology has not presented us with good theological reasons why we should not speak out against this gross perversion of the Christian faith. White theology has not been able to reshape the life of the white church so as to cleanse it of its racism and to liberate it from the iron claws of the white racist establishment of this nation. White theology has presented the Blacks a religion of contentment in the state of life in which they find themselves. Such an interpretation of the Christian faith avoided questions about personal dignity, collective power, freedom, equality, and self-determination. The white church establishment presented to the black people a religion carefully tailored to fit the purposes of the white oppressors, corrupted in language, interpretation, and application by the conscious and unconscious racism of white Christians from the first plantation missionary down to Billy Graham.

The white Christ of the white church establishment is the enemy of the black man. The teachings of this white Christ are used to justify wars, exploitation, segregation, discrimination, prejudice, and racism. This white Christ is the oppressor of the

---

[4] Vincent Harding, "Black Power and the American Christ," *The Black Power Revolt*, ed. Floyd B. Barbour (Boston: F. Porter Sargent, 1968), p. 86.

[5] Kyle Haselden, *The Racial Problem in Christian Perspective* (New York: Harper & Bros., 1959), pp. 42–43.

black man, and the black preacher and scholar was compelled to discover a Christ in his image of blackness. He was forced to look at the teachings of Jesus in the light of his own black experience and discover what this black Jesus said about the realities of his own life. The black preacher, seminary student, and scholar had their work cut out for them. If Bultmann's task was to demythologize the New Testament, the black preacher and scholar had to detheologize his mind of the racist ideas which had crept into interpretations of Jesus and to see him in the depth of his full humanity.

We remind you, we were asked to address ourselves "in the general area of understanding and communicating the Christian faith in today's revolutionary society." The first requirement is one of admitting the inadequacies of an understanding of the Christian faith which is used to support our contemporary racist society. Black and white scholars must read again the scriptures with new eyes and minds so as to hear the words of Jesus in their disturbing clarity.

The subject of all preaching is Jesus Christ. As Paul says, "We proclaim Christ—yes, Christ nailed to the cross; and though this is a stumbling-block to Jews and folly to Greeks, yet to those who have heard his call, Jews and Greeks alike, he is the power of God and the wisdom of God (1 Cor. 1:23–24, NEB)." [6]

## A RECOVERY OF THE HUMANITY OF JESUS

Detheologizing demands that we recover the humanity of Jesus in all its depth, length, breadth, and height. Jesus was born in a barn, wrapped in a blanket used for sick cattle, and placed in a stall. He died on a city dump outside Jerusalem.

The New Testament presents with disturbing clarity its record of the birth, ministry, and death of Jesus. There is no attempt to hide the stark realities which confronted Jesus from the barn of Bethlehem to the city dump of Jerusalem. The realism is naked and stark. Jesus was born in a barn. He died on a city dump. Even the place of the birth of Jesus is identified with the needs and the conditions of people. Where the need is

[6] From *The New English Bible, New Testament, op. cit.*

the deepest, the situation most desperate, and the pain the sharpest, that is precisely where Jesus is. We repeat, even in the birth of Jesus, the Gospels of Matthew and Luke identify him with the needs, the suffering, the pain, and the anxieties of the world. You see, most of the world's babies are not born in the palaces of kings or the government houses of prime ministers, or the manses of bishops. Most of the world's babies are born in the ghettos of corrupt cities, in mud houses, in disintegrated cottages with cracked floors and stuffed walls where the muffled cries of unattended mothers mingle with the screams of newborn infants.

Bultmann writes about the offense of the incarnation of the word.[7] He contends that the revealer appears not as man in general; that is, not simply as a bearer of human nature but as a definite human being in history—Jesus of Nazareth—a Jew. The humanity of Jesus is genuine humanity. The writer of the Gospel of John has no theory about the preexistent miraculous entrance into the world or of the legend of the virgin birth. You know this legend or myth is presented to us in the Gospels of Matthew and Luke. The writer of the Gospel of Mark, the evangelist of the Fourth Gospel, and Paul teach a high Christology without reference to the virgin birth.

Permit us to make this suggestion: Suppose we would omit the phrase "of the Holy Spirit" from Matthew 1:18 where it is recorded that "Mary had been betrothed to Joseph, before they came together she was found to be with child," what would this teach us about the humanity of Jesus? The reaction of many would be instantaneous and we would be accused of teaching "a doctrine of the illegitimate birth of Jesus." These objectors would insist that the birth of Jesus was due to a special act of God in and through humanity and that since Jesus is who he is and has done what he has done, this requires that his entrance into the world through humanity must be unique. Those who advocate this position forget the teachings of Jesus in particular and the New Testament writers in general concerning all life. Jesus taught that all life comes from God and that

---

[7] Rudolph Bultmann, *Theology of the New Testament,* Vol. II (London, SCM Press, 1955), pp. 40–41.

the birth of every child embodies and expresses a unique act of God.

Who Jesus was, was determined not necessarily by the manner of his birth but rather by what he did. John Knox states that the first form of the christological question was "What has God done through Jesus?" [8] The New Testament writers go to great length in presenting and discussing the saving deed of God through Jesus.

It was the belief of most writers of the New Testament that God was at work in the life and deeds of Jesus and that what God was doing in Jesus had both soteriological and eschatological significance. The conviction shared by most New Testament writers was to the effect that the last days had finally dawned and that God was acting decisively for man's salvation, renewal, and liberation. Again John Knox notes that the supreme importance of Jesus was determined more by his role and function than by his nature and further, "the christological question, which was originally a question about the eschatological and soteriological significance of an event, has become a question about the metaphysical nature of a person." [9] What must be done, therefore, if we are to understand the meaning and significance of Jesus, the Liberator, is to go behind the metaphysical speculation concerning him and ascertain and study those events which were foundational and believed by writers of the New Testament to possess saving and liberating significance. Men knew Jesus in terms of what he had done for them. J. K. Mozley states, "There is in the New Testament no speculative Christology divorced from the gospel of the Savior and the salvation he brings." [10] The early Christians were not seeking abstract definitions concerning the person of Jesus. The language of the early Christians was experiential, functional, and confessional. The foundation for the theology of Paul is the experience of what God had done for him in his own conversion,

[8] John Knox, *On the Meaning of Christ* (New York: Charles Scribner's Sons, 1947), p. 49.
[9] Ibid., pp. 55–56.
[10] J. K. Mozley, "Jesus in Relation to Believing Man," *Interpretation, A Journal of Bible and Theology* (January 1958), p. 11.

and he is basically interested in Jesus as the Redeemer, Revealer, and Liberator.

Brunner has argued that the titles given to Jesus in the New Testament are verbal in nature and character. They all describe an event, a work of God, or what God has done through Jesus in and for mankind. Further, Brunner writes: "Who and what Jesus is can only be stated at first at any rate by what God does and gives in him." [11]

Brunner insists that all christological titles must be understood not in terms of their substantive implications but in terms of their verbal functions. The term *Christos* may be interpreted as the one in whom and through whom God is to establish his sovereignty. The title *Son of God* is functional and it suggests an office and *the work* of the Liberator rather than a description of his metaphysical nature. Even the title *Immanuel* is defined in terms of its functional implications because this title means "God is with us." The title *Kyrios* describes the one who rules over the church. And finally, the title *Savior* points to the one who is to bring the healing, salvation, and liberation for which mankind yearns. [12]

The significance of Jesus for religious living is determined by what Jesus has done for mankind and all the christological titles applied to Jesus emphasize his gift of liberation to and for men. [13]

The divinity of Jesus is a divinity of service. His humanity was stretched in service so as to include the whole world of man in its miseries, slavery, frustration, and hopelessness. The New Testament word used to express this deep concern for men is *splagchnizesthai*. This word means to be moved with compassion, and it is used to describe an emotion which moved Jesus, the Liberator, at the very depth of his being. This word also indicates the depth of Jesus' concern and identification with others. Whenever the Gospel writers used this word

[11] Emil Brunner, *The Christian Doctrine of Creation and Redemption* (London: Lutterworth Press, 1952), p. 272.

[12] Ibid., p. 273.

[13] Ferdinand Hahn, *The Titles of Jesus in Christology* (New York: World Publishing Co., 1969), pp. 347–50; Oscar Cullmann, *The Christology of the New Testament* (London: SCM Press, 1959), pp. 3–6.

*splagchnizesthai* in reference to Jesus, they were attempting to describe the manner and the way in which Jesus identified himself completely with others and how he entered into the world of their misery and suffering, their slavery and hopelessness, and provided the means for liberation and renewal.

The men and women of the New Testament period who witness this ministry of service, love, and liberation reach the astounding conclusion that Jesus is the Revelation of a new kind of freedom and has made available to men the liberating power of God's love. Jesus is God acting in the service of men, thereby enabling them to realize their God-given potentials as human beings and as sons of God.

The Christians of the first century saw in Jesus, the Liberator, the answer to their most distressing problems. Jesus in his ministry, identifies himself with all men. The early Christians believed that he provided the answer to their most disturbing problems and whatever they needed he was sufficient. The writers of the four Gospels interpreted Jesus in the light of what they considered to be the greatest need of mankind. For the writer of the Gospel of Matthew, Jesus is the new Rabbi; for Luke, he is the great Physician; for Mark, he is the Stranger satisfying the deepest needs of men; and for John, Jesus is the Revealer.

The people of all races, because of his service, are able to identify with him and to see in his humanity, a reflection of their own images. Today the black man looks at Jesus—observes his ministry of love and liberation and considers him the black Messiah who fights oppression and sets the captive free.

## COMMITTED TO THE MESSAGE
## AND MISSION OF JESUS

The radicalness of the humanity of Jesus is not only expressed in his service but also in his speech. We must permit his speech to address, probe, disturb, and challenge us. Prof. Ernst Fuchs has called the rise of the gospel a speech event—an opening of a new dimension of man's awareness, a new breakthrough in language and symbolization. Professor Fuchs writes: "The early Church is itself a language phenomenon. It is precisely for this reason that it has created for itself a me-

morial in the new stylistic form of the Gospel. Even the
Apocalypse of John, and more than ever the apostolic epistles,
are creations of a new language that transforms everything with
which it comes into contact." [14]

The words of Jesus have the rugged fiber of a cypress
tree and the jagged edge of the crosscut saw. His language is
extreme, extravagant, explosive as hand grenades which are
tossed into the crowds that listened to him. A tremendous vigor
and vitality surges through his words. In Jesus' words, "A
man with a log in his eye tries to pick a cinder out of his
brother's eye." In the words of Jesus "a giant hand hangs a
millstone around the neck of one who exploits a little child and
hurls the sinner into the midst of the sea." In the words of
Jesus, "a man asks for bread and is given a stone, another asks
for fish and is given a snake." In the words of Jesus, "men
strain at the little gnats and gulp down the camels." In the
words of Jesus, "a mountain develops feet and casts itself into
the sea." He attacks the religious establishment of his day—
the religious leaders, the ordained ministers with such phrases
as "you hypocrites," "you blind guides," "you blind Pharisees,"
"you brood of snakes," "you serpents," "you murderers."

*Jesus spoke with authority and with power!*

In the city of Nazareth where he was reared, this dark,
long-haired, bearded ghetto lad of Nazareth took over the synagogue service and read his universal manifesto of liberation:

> The spirit of the Lord is upon me because he has anointed me;
> he has sent me to announce good news to the poor,
> to proclaim release for prisoners and recovery of sight for the
> blind;
> to let the broken victims go free,
> to proclaim the year of the Lord's favour (Luke 4:18–19,
> NEB).[15]

The reading of this liberation manifesto caused debates,
rebuttals, accusations, counterrebuttals, wrath, anger, and
hate. The Gospel of Luke is explicit in describing the reaction
of the religious establishment to the manifesto of liberation of
Jesus. "When they heard this, all in the synagogue were filled

---

[14] Ernst Fuchs, *Studies of the Historical Jesus* (Napierville, Ill.: Alec R.
Allenson, Inc., 1960), p. 68.
[15] From *The New English Bible, New Testament, op. cit.*

with wrath. And they rose up and put him out of the city, and led him to the brow of the hill on which their city was built, that they might throw him down headlong. But passing through the midst of them he went away (Luke 4:28–30)."

Liberation was the aim and the goal of the life of Jesus in the world. Liberation expresses the essential thrust of his ministry. The stage of his ministry was the streets. His congregation consisted of those who were written-off by the established church and the state. He ministered to those who needed him, "the nobodies of the world," the sick, the blind, the lame, and the demon-possessed. He invaded the chambers of sickness and death and hallowed these with the healing words of health and life. He invaded the minds of the demon-possessed and in those dark chambers of night he brought light, sanity, and order. Jesus ministered to men in their sorrow, sin, and degradation and offered them hope and light and courage and strength. He offered comfort to the poor who did not fit into the structure of the world. Jesus comforted the mourner and offered hope to the humble. He had a message for the men and women who had been pushed to the limits of human existence and on these he pronounced his blessedness.

The people who received help from Jesus are throughout the Gospels on the fringe of society—men who because of fate, guilt, and prejudices were considered marked men; *sick people,* who must bear their disease as punishment for crime or for some sin committed; *demoniacs,* that is those possessed of demons; *the lepers,* the first-born of death to whom fellowship was denied; *gentiles,* women and children who did not count for anything in the community, and *the really bad people,* the prostitutes, the thieves, the murderers, the robbers. When Jesus was pressed for an explanation of the radicalness of the thrust of his ministry, his answer was simple and direct. "Those who are well have no need of a physician, but those who are sick; I have not come to call the righteous, but sinners (Luke 5:31–32)."

The greatness of Jesus is to be found precisely in the way in which he makes himself accessible to those who need him, ignoring conventional limitations and issuing that grand and glorious welcome—"Come unto me all ye that labor and are heavy laden and I will give you rest."

The Gospel of Mark records the healing of Peter's mother-in-law. Please listen to this passage. "And immediately he left the synagogue, and entered the house of Simon and Andrew, with James and John. Now Simon's mother-in-law lay sick with a fever, and immediately they told him of her (Mark 1:29–30)." Now, verse 31 tells us what Jesus did: "And he came and took her by the hand and lifted her up, and the fever left her; and she served them."

Jesus is saying to his disciples the only way to lift is to touch. You cannot lift men without touching them. Jesus is saying to the church—the people of God—the church must not be locked in its stained-glass fortress with its multicolored windows, red-cushioned seats, crimson carpets, and temperature-controlled auditorium where according to Kierkegaard, "An anemic preacher preaches anemic gospel about an anemic Christ to an anemic congregation." [16]

The church building must be a point of departure, a departure into the world, into the dirty here and now.

We are challenged to continue in our world Jesus' ministry of love and liberation. We must recognize that to be a Christian is to be contemporaneous with Jesus, the Liberator. To be sure, to be a Christian is not to hold views about Jesus but rather to become a contemporary with Jesus in his ministry of suffering and humiliation and of love and liberation. To be a Christian is to be committed to the man Jesus in spite of the world's rejection of him, in spite of Christendom's betrayal of him, and in spite of the social and intellectual stigma involved in accepting and following him. To be a Christian is to stand with Jesus and participate in his ministry of love and liberation at the crossways of the world where men are crucified on the crosses of poverty, racism, war, and exploitation. To be a Christian is to try again to introduce Christianity into Christendom and to set free again the powers of the love and liberating ministry of Jesus, the Liberator.

[16] Sören Kierkegaard, *Attack upon Christendom*, tr. by Walter Lowrie (Princeton: Princeton University Press, 1946), p. 30.